VALUE FROM SECURITY

David Burrill & Kevin Green

authorHOUSE®

AuthorHouse™ UK Ltd.
500 Avebury Boulevard
Central Milton Keynes, MK9 2BE
www.authorhouse.co.uk
Phone: 08001974150

First published by AuthorHouse 5/17/2011

ISBN: 978-1-4520-7331-6 (sc)

Contents

Forewords

1.

A decade ago, we were dealing with serious but new concerns. These included discussions about what the Internet might mean for us, well before anyone put the one billion plus current users in 2010 figure in any sound forecast. We had Y2K, or the Millennium Bug, threatening to bring civilisation to its knees, and certainly accounting for some millennium sized prophylactic budgets. We saw the return to China of Hong Kong, and questions about the impact of that on economic development in the region. There was even a feeling in some quarters, as Mr Francis Fukuyama indicated in his book, that we were reaching a period known as 'The End of History'.[1]

Since those days of what looked like an end-of-century confidence, we have now become familiar with new, let's call them, Brands of Distinction, of varying qualities, half of which were only dreams 10 years ago. From Google to the i-Pod, we have come into a whole new digital world. From ExxonMobil, who then delivered the world's highest ever profits, regarded in some circles as one of the top 10 companies to work for, and regarded in other circles as a pariah in a Warming World, to Enron, one of the biggest dramas ever staged, and a pure fiction. From Al-Qaeda and Guantanamo Bay to Swine Flu and Harry Potter, the 13 October 2008 and onwards financial maelstrom, and the USA's first black President.

We live in a world of speed and connectivity that binds us globally, and whose formerly distant-seeming events now affect us as they actually happen, often on the screens we so regularly have in front of us. In what Thomas Friedman called 'the Flat World', the reality of the globally interdependent market hits us face on every minute. Who would have known all that was coming?

In fact, since the 1990s, we have all become more aware that we live in a world of simultaneous multiple agendas and events, all of which can be really 'up-close and personal', yet not in old Coca Cola's Utopian view of being "in perfect harmony". Through this period, organisations like the European Round Table of Industrialists have played an important role in partnership with senior delegates of The Commission, Europol and academic institutions, on pioneering security initiatives. There has been significant involvement in an increasing number of EU driven public and private partnership programs and conferences concerned with business security challenges and crime prevention strategies. Of course, what we do in 'our' region also in its turn has its impact on the larger world stage

Today, the role and value of the security management professional, and profession, to business, the media, government agencies and the general public, has never been so much in the spotlight. We really are in a world where corporate security is to corporations what national security is to nation-states.

In some nations there is a sense that national identity is in decline, where in others it is nascent. Other forms of identity that unite, steer and drive behaviour and attitudes are also fighting for their share of hearts and minds.

There are always surprises. News from the UK revealed that Roman Catholicism appears to be a growing religion today, bolstered by significant immigration from formerly far away countries and communities. Berlin is now the most populous Turkish city in the European Union. Iran has, relatively, the youngest population in the world, with over 40% of its population under the age of 15. And the EU, with nearly 30 states, is moulding an identity in parallel to those of its members. All these kinds of demographics and tectonic shifts create continuous uncertainties for societies and citizens.

Within this spinning whirl of a world, corporate security management has had to expand and embrace these kinds of statistics and complexities as each year unfolds. As with Moore's law of doubling data density and halving costs at an alarming rate, the same pressures appear to apply to security professionals and their advisors. The message comes in annually – "Manage more for proportionally, or actually, less".

Many of you will share the view that to go on treating security simply as a cost of doing business should not be regarded as a realistic basis for judging its potential contribution to modern enterprises. What we mean is that, beyond security's obligation to provide benchmarked levels of asset protection to organisations, security management in the 21st century should really and justifiably be able to handle two further elements.

The first extra element is to be duty bound to discover and deliver more, and measurable, value to the enterprises it serves. This is not just in terms of monetary contributions, valuable as they can be, but also in terms of more intangible values, like reputation and good will.

The second extra element should be to champion a push against what might be described as a fetish for complexity that obfuscates the ability to provide simple, workable, and accountable solutions in many organisations. Contrary to perceptions, security can be a core support for transparency, more of which is truly needed.

But there is always a way to go. There is a need to increase the effectiveness and productivity of security professionals with more educational programmes and materials that address overall management issues as well as broad security interests. There is the growing need to improve the ways in which crimes originating inside corporations are identified and handled within cultures which themselves appear to tolerate such behaviour. The more security becomes an integrated business function, the better the organisation's value, and values.

Security is everywhere. It is ubiquitous. In fact, security may be one of the last remaining areas of unexplored incremental value across entire operations. Think about that. Security may be a great multiplier, if only we can find mature ways to share and co-operate across professional functions. The core challenge is to work out how that may be achieved. Security will continue to develop into a star-billing player at the highest levels of organisations, as security issues and events continue to emerge to challenge the identities, reputations, and values of citizens, corporations, and nation states themselves.

We must work to improve management's sensitivity towards security's potential role and contribution. Corporate executives of large, leading enterprises recognise the need to be in control regarding security related risks. We need to ensure this cascades through all professional enterprises, and in stakeholder and opinion forming and influencing communities.

We cannot tell you the names of the next decades' most famous brands or characters, but we can tell you this – There has never been a better time to work in a world where the question "Is security really worth it?" has such profound implications, and must be answered with a resounding "Yes, and here's why..."

Extracts from a speech prepared by Burrill Green for the American Society of Industrial Security, Europe (and delivered in Berlin, March 2007)

2.

We would like to propose that this book is a most timely contribution to the need for an expanded role and understanding of the contribution that professional corporate security can bring to organisations at a time when we have seen an unprecedented amount of damage caused by risky, reckless, and often illegal behaviour, particularly recently, in financial services sectors of the economy.

A number of critical events have taken place, from the collapse of major institutions to the workings of notorious individuals, that should inspire surviving enterprises to embrace the need for thorough ethical practices, but of course there are still organisations that are reluctant to receive and address these messages. There will always be people out there who will rationalise what's going on and still say "But our own people wouldn't do that". It's still going to happen.

One survey we were able to review showed that some 63% of executives expected accounting fraud to increase during the next two years because of the recession. Many companies paid lip-service to ethics and compliance but pushed them aside, or even fired their representatives, when major revenue-generating decisions were taken. The revenue generation often disappeared entirely.

We know from those players who have a strong commitment to ethics and transparency, that there is also a strong correlation with positive financial results. Proper assessments of behaviour on these kinds of dimensions cannot be conducted through elementary tick-box surveys. Truly valuable analyses also involve capturing a deep understanding of ethical issues within specific operating cultures and environments. Greed is only one clear manifestation of behaviour, and is an elemental part of the capitalistic systems we have condoned in our society – this will not disappear, and those for whom the opportunity to make money quickly, combined with the skills to do it, arises, will still appear on the scene. We must recognise this is a fundamental trait of behaviour.

Having acknowledged that, we don't, and shouldn't have to run away from the fact. Professional corporate security, practised responsibly, helps avoid ethical disasters by supporting good and able leadership, which in turn sets laudable behaviour with no sacrifice of desirable values.

There are plenty of first-class books and advisors on how to harness the technical array of security tools and services that are available to organisations to protect themselves and others. This book looks at issues and challenges from a wider range of perspectives, and is realistic in its honesty at portraying human fallibility, and how to manage this fact. In learning more about how security, when it is integrated into a business, and where its leading practitioners are core members of cross-functional management teams, can become a value generator, we come to see that corporate security is capable of becoming a core asset, with long-term value. Leading corporate security players are in the business of enhancing performance, not reining it in. A few naysayers who resist all forms of boundaries to their profit generation schemes may find some surprising elements of practical support for their continuation and ethically positive survival in these pages.

Burrill Green
2010

For more information about us, or to engage further in this arena of adding value to security, please go to our websites at:

www.burrillgreen.com **and** www.secureleadership.com

Preface

The more you seek security, the less of it you have. But the more you seek opportunity, the more likely it is that you will achieve the security you desire.[1]

In reading this book, if you are a committed seeker of value for your organisation, we hope you will discover fresh perspectives within our theme of *Value from Security*. If you are currently a security professional, or someone who has responsibility for overall security within your portfolio of responsibilities, then we hope you will also find fresh things to look at and respond to. If you are a shareholder, you will find ways to discover whether security is providing all it can to protect and nurture your interests. The aim is for value to sit alongside protection as security's core contributions to enterprise.

The book is deliberately written from a number of perspectives for two reasons:

- One, to demonstrate the value of being able to have a broader vision about the drivers and motivations of professionals, stakeholders and influencers where corporate security can play an enhanced role

- Two, to show that it is only through networked sharing that the true value and potential of our proposed form of security can be realised throughout an organisation.

We demonstrate what has led to the status of security today across many fields of operation, what is affecting current thinking and behaviour in successful enterprises, and what may come to represent the general acceptance of security's contribution and value in the coming years.

Value from Security doesn't simply mean monetary value. Value applies equally to the ways in which security can contribute to corporate responsibility and reputation. This double delivery, which we can also term 'profitable security', should also manifest itself in ways that anyone in an organisation can access and understand. In the generally accepted view that organisations have different and identifiable cultures, one of the contributing parts to that overall culture is the role of the discrete yet integrated security function.

As an example of using different perspectives for a moment, consider the research studies of what makes up the universe we live in. There is apparently a large amount of 'dark matter' in it, which might account for projections about missing or invisible material matter. This dark matter appears to be quintessential, and helps hold everything else together.[2] We want to show how integrated business security can play a similar seamless and vital role in helping hold together the positive role of successful international organisational cultures and their products and services. Clearly there are at least two ways of regarding security as dark matter.

In fast-moving modern businesses today, as at Cisco Systems for example, there is increasingly a definable culture of security that touches all parts of the organisation, and is a fully integrated part of the business. Indeed, security's strategy, goals and processes are derived from the core of the operating business itself, and security is a critical success factor in the eyes of everyone from the CEO, through the organisation, and beyond, to partners and suppliers, clients and customers.

It is only recently, within a decade, that the idea of a pervasive security culture in non-military or national security organisations, where everyone feels a sense of ownership and accountability, has gained significant ground and supporting practitioners.

As this idea has been fostered, the role of a Chief Security Officer (CSO) has also evolved into one of embracing the role of communications evangelist, not just a keeper of the keys, who is increasingly recruited for, and assessed on, the ability to embed security in a wider organisational culture. This same person may well also hold a different title, like Head of Corporate Affairs, Head of Legal, or Head of Human Resources. This embracing of the security function by other stakeholders and senior executive officers will continue. Generalist and broad management skills will be required in addition to technical security competences, as value seekers make more demands of the previously bolted on security function. Security, 'the stuff', isn't just out there – it's a key part of the total organisational universe. It's ubiquitous.

In Fortune 500 firms, a study showed that security leaders need to develop "composite security metrics that are simple to understand and clearly linked to the business" and that these have become primary imperatives[3]. The Massachusetts Institute of Technology in another piece of research asked over 1200 people from six companies what their assessment of readiness to combat specific types of security risk was, and the perceived importance of that risk, utilising a TQM (Total Quality Management) methodology approach. Critical in the study was the drive to understand better how 'perceptions shape decisions'.[4] The study showed that today there are still significant gaps between the importance of security risks and the readiness, ability and awareness of the need to address those risks. The security risk areas included security culture and policy itself, accessibility, vulnerability, confidentiality, financial and IT resources, and business strategy.

Any senior manager with no link to any of these issues is surely a rare being, so the likelihood is that managers could do well from contributing to the closing of such gaps, and the generation and elevation of security as a quintessential element of corporate culture, not something that can be sidelined for convenience when a big deal suddenly arises.

The real challenge is getting more people to see this, and then to act on it. It is not easy, and it takes time. We aim to make these steps more palatable to all parties, but accept that Schopenhauer's observation holds true not just for scientists – "All truth passes through three stages. First, it is ridiculed. Second, it is violently opposed. Third, it is accepted as being self-evident."[5]

Even in a positive world, the overestimation of how secure an organisation and its assets are is commonplace. But we are not suggesting doom-mongering as a viable style of raising the awareness of security considerations. We aim to demonstrate how more active and conscious participation by stakeholders to improve security throughout an organisation can be achieved pragmatically:

- Job One is to ensure that security's role as an asset protector is assured.
- Job Two is to see how security can perform an additional undiluted role as an incremental source of profit and other profitable values.

This also means that whoever has the remit of providing security leadership can no longer behave simply as a compliance tactician. A pro-active security leader will best serve a company through two developments – his or her own improved operating skills, and a balance through direct links to a supportive CEO and across all key company functions.

The Chief Information Officer of Cisco[5] said, "When reporting solely to IT, all a chief security officer's time could be consumed by operational issues. Reporting simply to the CEO can also be an opportunity to overturn security guidelines in favour of the bottom line only … a dual structure maintains both a balance, and independence, which lends a new meaning to the notion of objective risk management".

What we are talking about in this book has been put into successful practice by us. It is not theory or wishful thinking, but the summary of actions by people who have spent a long time building experiences that today we call best practice.

Kevin Green and David Burrill
Burrill Green
2010

www.burrillgreen.com **and** www.secureleadership.com

Book Structure

Since much of security is about perception and perspectives, we invite you to read the whole dialogue in the book for the most rounded view. This will give you a clearer idea about what it is like to work with security issues and opportunities from different positions inside and outside organisations. It may help refine how your contribution to and support for security becoming a more valuable and profitable practice can be enhanced.

If you don't have time or the desire for that, just cherry-pick from the headings that might ring bells for you. As far as we are concerned, you can get higher Value from Security wherever your starting point or position, and we offer here ways to treat the role of security as a virtuous circle – things may look different from where you are standing, but you're still connected to everyone and everything else.

Aim and Scope

Today, in a globally insecure world, security should be a key driver of value. All too often, corporate security is not consistently linked to core strategic organisational areas like business building and strategic planning. A lack of measures and metrics to quantify its contribution has slowed down its chances to earn a rightful place at the top table. Where world-class companies have embraced an approach to security as a 'value adding' function, significant business and organisational benefits have emerged. These include productivity gains, new revenue opportunities, and improved corporate reputation and resilience. Security needs to change in this way in more organisations:

It is time for more people to have the opportunity to discover how security can perform a transformational role, not simply a passive one.

We show what security's real capabilities are, and what needs to be done to realise them. The experiences presented have occurred in real organisations, globally, that are reaping the rewards of being at the vanguard of this new approach to corporate security management. The book has clear messages for those practitioners at the core of security functions today. As importantly, there are practical and value generating reasons for other functional and cross functional heads of organisations to review the fresh perspectives presented here. Security can and should be business driven and not compliance driven. We would like to see more leaders show commitment to security as a core business value, and we show the steps that can be taken to make this desire an actuality. To make this change there are profound implications for the kinds of people who are in security roles, and who might be in them in the future, and we explain what will be required to fulfil security's new role as a business enabler.

The book's core target is seekers of value for organisations and investments, with especial emphasis on those who have security remits. Management teams and shareholders will come to realise that:

Security is a significant area of unrealised incremental value today.

Chapters

1. Security in Business – Cost or Contributor?

We believe it is time to reconcile a number of opposing views and beliefs about the role of security in the corporate solar system. Is it simply a cost of doing business, a boring necessity, a way to get boxes ticked in frameworks of regulation and compliance, or can it be seen as an elemental force positively influencing an entire corporate space? What is driving the development of views, and what is the new universe going to look like?

2. Corruption and Closed Minds

Professional security management should play a core role in crafting the links between the ways a company or organisation does its business, the quality and the depth of its relationships with the community, and its ability to operate in a safe and sustainable way. People should not be denied access to quality products and services, wherever they are. Security can play a major role in what will continue to be debates and action about intellectual property, rights, authenticity, transparency, and value. What this chapter moves towards is the idea of opening minds more, so that good practices can be adopted by a wider range of people, for a wider range of benefits.

3. A Fresh Start – Outset Security

What we explore will help you see how security can play an enhanced role in the overall context and life of an organisation. We look at how security can be a profit contributor and business enabler, without detriment to its expected role as a protective agent. We introduce the idea of how outset security can further support an organisation's values and reputation. Getting there requires certain changes in thinking and practice, which also means revising views and notions about the old established order, or world of security.

4. Making Security a Competitive Asset

For global and multinational organisations, operational challenges have never been so demanding. The means to attack or destroy value have never been so cheap, deep and relentless. For specialists in security management, there is a need to reinforce security's core role in the coming years, enhancing its ability to make a significant contribution as an integrated business function.

The mission is to make security management a competitive asset.

There are two sides to this:

- One is to ensure that security provides an organisation with the most resilient platform for protecting its interests and assets.
- The other side is to use security to deliver increased value.

What critical factors will affect companies trying to be competitive over the next decade? What is the feasibility and relevance of security in addressing these challenges? In answering these questions, we re-enter the world of intangible as well as tangible value.

Security has a significant role to play in debates along the lines of, "Who audits the auditors?" This could be a whole book to itself, but here we simply outline the need for a closer look at the case and the debates that should be happening. Likewise, in addition to supporting the process of mergers and acquisition (M&A) activity through risk management fundamentals, security has an ongoing role to play in supporting the branding and reputation of merging entities, and security should be judged by the extent of its presence in such strategic issues, not by its absence or 'presence by afterthought'. This is another example of business outset security in a specific application.There is a strategic need to capture actionable data and translate it into knowledge that will have both a commercial value and that will enhance corporate reputation.

5. Security and Shareholder Value

6. Getting Even More from Your Investment in Security

Working globally, with many of the world's largest and most respected companies, we share proven experiences and practices that can help an organisation realise incremental benefits and value from a shift in the way investment in security is regarded.

7. Achieving a Secure Advantage

We believe security management is functionally in a key position in an organisation to meet unthinkable and unexpected challenges. We need to redefine 'uncertainty' in terms of consequences and capabilities.

Management teams need to know which critical factors will help keep business competitive in the months and years to come. Knowing what the implications of these factors are has a crucial influence on designing and configuring the business and its supporting organisation. The feasibility and relevance of security applications in addressing these factors and challenges is a strategic issue, globally.

8. Making Security Make Sense

As with nation states, no effective security management portfolio can successfully operate outside the cultural context of the host. It is essential to become familiar with this critical yet intangible dimension. The best solutions will only emerge from recognising how this approach and insight will help realise the most effective bespoke fit for a particular environment.

Does the version of a secure environment, from your position, look the same as it does to others around you? It's worth reflecting that each generation is driven by unique ideas about security. That means that the different generational experiences and values of those around us shape our needs, so unless you are in an environment where you are only surrounded by your peers, it becomes important to understand that the motives of each generation can also be used to help make approaches to developing a successful security strategy more successful.

Both nation states and multinationals share needs and compete simultaneously. Greater opportunities bring greater risks, as the spectacular collapse of 'Icarus-like' business models testifies, or risk-taking at the state level backfires. To avoid clashes between open-source giants and entrenched corporate and state organisations, there is a need to understand more about the benefits that can be developed through co-operation. To do this requires an acceptance that security has an important role to play in supporting further empowerment, and that this must be a shared resource.

9. Security Leadership

In this chapter we concentrate on what best demonstrates the most rounded set of skills to enable security to deliver more value. We launch a series of views and projections about what the future security leader or team might look like, where he or she or they might come from, and what they will all be expected to do.

What are the required characteristics of the new security leader, and leadership?

10. Further Perspectives on the Changing Role of Corporate Security

Have there been significant signs, gradual in their nature, which we have barely noticed but which have been changing our lives and the lives of those around us? We are not in the soothsaying business, but we do believe that preparing for the unexpected today is a sound way of working towards a future over which better quality control can be achieved.

This provides the bridge for discussing the skills security leaders will need to hone and develop, and the way to measure and design a profitable security organisation to move forward.

11. Standards in Security: Do You Measure Up?

What measures or metrics can be applied to help demonstrate to management and other interested parties that security is bringing value to an organisation? This is a primer with pointers to significant sources of technical expertise and references.

12. Designing a Profitable Multi-Functional Security Organisation

Here we look further at ways to engage people and how to make sure the best areas of opportunity for an environment can be designed and implemented, in the context of a background of continual change and challenges. Again it is a pointer towards other sources of detailed technical support and practice.

13. Security as a Brand

In the same way that brands permeate every area and aspect of the companies that own and nurture them, security is displaying family likenesses to brands and brand values. Brands are all about trust, and security is no different. Brands can also be said to be the sum total of the information people carry around in their heads about them, and the experiences they have had with them. Brands do not exist in a merely physical form. Neither does security. We look briefly at the idea of marketing security as a brand.

14. Secure Advantage Summary

15. Security Principles and Key Points

This book has been driven by a set of principles that fundamentally underline our approach and attitude to the contemporary business of delivering Value from Security. Whether you read the book from cover to cover or cut straight to this chapter, you will now find the summary of our principles and the key messages the book is putting out, derived from all the practical experience and examples we have set out in the preceding chapters

Notes, References and Acknowledgements

Clearly the world will continue to change. Here we part with just a few more thoughts about what we have done, some thoughts from other experts, and how we have got to where we have today. Further thoughts will no doubt be added as future editions come out to include and respond to developments and events.

Biographical Details

The authors are David Burrill and Kevin Green, and short biographies are included here:

David Burrill – has been a professional international Intelligence and Security operator/ manager for most of his professional life. On retiring from the military in 1992, having held the appointment of Deputy Director Intelligence Corps, and Chief of Staff Intelligence and Security Centre of the UK Armed Forces, he joined BAT Industries, a major global insurance and tobacco conglomerate, and subsequently on de-merger, British American Tobacco (the world's second largest quoted tobacco organisation – with presence in 180+ countries), as Head of Security. David, who is a Freeman of the City of London, has had close and regular contact with the private security sector for over 26 years. His military connections have continued and he has etired as the Deputy Colonel Commandant of the UK's Army Intelligence Corps.

A graduate of the Royal Military Academy Sandhurst, the Army Command and Staff Course and the Open University, he has been a Defence Fellow of London University and is a Fellow of three British professional institutes: The Chartered Institute of Management, The Chartered Institute of Personnel Development, and The Security Institute. A member of the globally prestigious International Security Management Association, he was, from June 1998 to June 1999, its President (the first non North American to hold the position). David is also an emeritus member of the UK's Risk and Security Management Forum.

In 2003, David Burrill became the first co-Chairman of the UK Foreign and Commonwealth Office's Security Information Service for Business Overseas (SISBO) – a public/private sector partnership initiative of which he was one of the key architects. David Burrill was awarded an OBE in the 2004 New Years Honours List for services to international security management. In April 2005, David was honoured by *CSO Journal* with a Compass Award for visionary leadership, and by ASIS International as the first recipient of its European Leadership Award.

In November 2005 he became the first foreigner to receive a distinguished achievement award from the Overseas Security Advisory Council of the US Department of State, and is the first foreigner to be granted Alumni status of the distinguished council. In July 2006, he was recognised by the Association of Security Consultants with the award of the Imbert Prize for distinguished achievement from citations submitted by ASIS International, the British Security Industry Association, and The Security Institute.

Kevin Green – a graduate of Trinity College, Cambridge, has worked in public and private sector enterprises for more than a quarter of a century. He has specialised in the development of strategies to achieve new levels of growth, efficiency and organisation. As a practitioner within organisations, and as a third party advisor, he has acquired a rounded perspective on organisational needs and behaviour.

The first part of his career saw Kevin working in marketing communications, companies including spells with specialists like Foote, Cone and Belding, WPP at Y&R and JWT, and Havas Euro RSCG. These assignments demanded frequent travel. His experience drew him to working internationally from city bases like London, Amsterdam, Paris, and Madrid, serving a diverse range of globally-operating blue-chip companies. These have included technology-focused operators like Hewlett-Packard, Kodak, Philips, Xerox, and Unisys; fast-moving consumer goods manufacturers from food and personal products like Colgate-Palmolive, Kraft General Foods, Mars, Nestle, Procter & Gamble and Unilever, through to car-makers like Mercedes, Peugeot-Citroen and Volvo; and finally, service providers ranging from local government to utilities.

He has worked frequently with teams to develop new products and services, and marketing support portfolios for them. This work has been coupled with a career-long interest in training, coaching, and development. Kevin continues to work on helping organisations identify, create and realise additional value from their core assets.

As E M Forster left it, "Only connect..."[1]

Introduction

Many opportunities are overlooked by companies that are too narrowly focused on a particular definition of what business they are in. An opportunity is not there until after you have seen it. Seeking, recognising and designing opportunities requires a different set of thinking skills.[1]

Today, in a globally insecure world, only a small proportion of companies regard security as a key driver of added value. Corporate security is not consistently linked to core strategic organisational areas like business development and strategic planning. A lack of measures and metrics to quantify its contribution has slowed down its chances to earn a rightful place at the top table. Its adoption is all too often a result of incentives from governments forced to introduce more regulation and compliance in fields like financial services.Yet in those areas that have embraced a professional approach to regarding security as a 'value adding' function, significant business and organisational benefits have emerged. These include productivity gains, the prevention of potential crises, new revenue opportunities, and improved corporate reputation and resilience.[2]

We will show what can happen when security is able to move beyond the constraining and occasionally dismissive view that it is merely a cost of doing business, and that utilised properly, it can become a trusted value driver. More than that, the experiences discussed here have really occurred in organisations, around the world. These enterprises are reaping the rewards of being at the vanguard of this new approach to security. The prospect of supporting profit on both the bottom line and on the overall values of an organisation is significant, and measurable.

While this book has clear messages for those practitioners at the core of what are regarded as security functions today, there are also practical reasons for other functional and cross functional heads of organisations, stakeholders and opinion formers, to review the fresh perspectives presented here.

Security can and should be business driven and not compliance driven.

Our approach to security's role enhances standards of compliance where it is practiced, and it also works as a creator of incremental benefits. We would like to see more leaders show commitment to security as a core business value, and we show the steps that can be taken to make this desire become an actuality. Security should no longer be seen as 'a level of inconvenience'. To make this change there are profound implications for the kinds of people who are in security roles, and who might be in them in the future, and we will explain what will be required to fulfil security's new role as an enabler, not just a passive player.

There are a number of excellent providers of services for specific security technical issues and challenges, processes and programmes, who can support and execute many of the things we propose. Our purpose is not to provide lots of checklists and technical data in the main body of the work, but to promote discussion within a wide arena of the benefits of treating security as a deliverer of incremental value.

However, should you want to pursue the services of some of these outstanding people, or contribute your own experience and recommendations to the debate, visit our operations at www.burrillgreen.com and www.secureleadership.com where we disclose many of our own recommended associates and partners, technical expertise and supporting resources.

If you want more Value from Security, here's a starting place from which to journey.

Security can and should be business driven and not compliance driven.

---

1. Security in Business – Cost or Contributor?

We believe it is time to reconcile a number of opposing views and beliefs about the role of security in the corporate solar system. Is it simply a cost of doing business, a boring necessity, a way to get boxes ticked in frameworks of regulation and compliance, or can it be seen as an elemental force positively influencing an entire corporate space? What is driving the development of views, and what is the new universe going to look like?

There are few books about business that don't say somewhere how we are all living in a world of change. Some sow the seeds of urgency by noting how we are in a world of accelerating rates of change. Others settle for the old oriental approach of declaring that change is the only constant we can be sure of. For every new perspective, new lenses are crafted to see what all this change amounts to. The books and the readers of signs try to stay on top of things, trying to look beyond horizons, to anticipate tomorrows. It's only human nature to want to feel there is some control over eventualities, so there will always be a market creating new concepts to deal with expectations seen and unforeseen, like 'managing uncertainty'.

The very act of categorising things appears to help many people reduce fear. This understanding has served religions well for millennia, and fuels New Age alternatives today. People also feel that by counting and measuring we can come to know enough to feel reassured about the context we live in. These processes and behaviours are simply other ways in which many people try to structure the world they encounter, to make it make sense, to fathom it, as an older measurer might have pronounced.

Security, "the state of being or feeling secure"[1], is usually also regarded as being a means of reducing uncertainty, although security practitioners are always there to point out that 100% security can never be achieved.

Making idealised promises can lead to seriously negative outcomes for all involved. For example, greyhounds beyond their racing best in the UK were promised a 'secure future' as their owners handed them over to a re-homing facility. This, for the dogs handed over to this particular place, sadly meant an almost immediate death, and it was years before owners new what the 100% guarantee of a 'secure future' was really about. It is not the kind of guarantee of security we would endorse.

Security is as much an emotional state as a physical one, an intangible, which makes counters and measurers shy of its overall features. Security, unlike cash flow, has flaws and uncertainties, which doesn't appear to enhance its position and promise. In a world of numbers-fuelled ambition and achievement, how can you take something seriously when its very existence demands the acknowledgement of its opposite – insecurity and imperfection?

Often, security appears to start from the wrong base. How can you justify and measure the absence of something like non-delivered or executed threats, versus the clear delivery and presence of something – cash in the bank, or food on the table, as a profitable result?

There was a retirement party for a fireman at London's Heathrow Airport. After 35 years of service, he had never been in a call-out that had resulted in a loss of life. All that training and investment had led to 'nothing'. That was one perspective. Or maybe it led to everything. It depends how you value the absence of something. It also depends on what you consider to be values. It is time to take security and see how it relates to the corporate solar system, to see whether corporate security is some kind of planet or world, living largely unto itself and with only a vague co-dependency on others, or whether it is something altogether different, like the 'dark matter' we talked about earlier, a force, or an energy, with a different role than was previously thought about, or recognised, by observers and measurers. Why?

It is time to reconcile a number of opposing views and beliefs about the role of security. If it is not simply a cost of doing business, a boring necessity, a way to get boxes ticked in frameworks of regulation and compliance, how can it be seen as an elemental force positively influencing an entire corporate space? What is driving the development of views, and what is the new universe going to look like?

- At the macro level, security and security related issues are becoming more pervasive in society.

- Security is seen as a price to pay for freedom, not as a value intrinsic to it. Franklin D Roosevelt's four freedoms of democracy were of speech, of worship, from want, and from fear.

- Security has not been treated by management with the same rigour and respect as other corporate functions, because it hasn't, in many cases, been regarded as a core, or strategic function. This is both a failure in reasoning about its capability, and a failure to market it properly within organisations. It is also a failure of a number of people who have been unwilling or unable to bring their experience and skills into the heart of contemporary corporate cultures, which may be different from those they experienced in former roles or in very different kinds of cultural contexts.

- Security, and the responsibilities that derive from it, is now affecting more people in the workplace than ever before, from those with legal obligations to those who thought security was a job someone else took care of.

- Security will increasingly have to manage emotional and intangible factors, becoming *values*-driven, not merely value-driven.

- Security professionals will need to demonstrate skills in influence and imagination that have in the past been secondary to specific security craft skills.

- The whole business of Social Intelligence, the new neuroscience basis for looking at human relationships and interaction, and a move on from the older and better-known ideas of Emotional Intelligence, will become essential knowledge for those whose professional business is to understand how people function, what drives them, and how their motivations are made manifest.

4

- Security will develop as a brand value, and will need to be managed as a brand. While brands may be metaphors for all the perceptions and associations we carry around in our heads about them, a common feature in all those brands we rate is the extent to which we are prepared to credit them with the notion of trust and trusted-ness.
- Management teams and shareholders will come to realise that:

Security is a significant area of unrealised incremental value today.

Let's look at some developments that may surprise those not close to certain specialised applications.

In emerging markets, a modern approach to, and the utilisation of, corporate security, has played a key role in companies' successes. This has often been driven by the need to use security to become more competitive, as opposed to using it to defend bastions rooted only in the past. Multinational companies from markets like China, Mexico, Argentina and Brasil are building number one share positions and enviable reputations in advanced product fields, from semiconductors to regional commercial jet planes. A competitive edge with these players didn't arise simply because they had unrestricted access to natural resources or cheap labour. Things didn't grow just from a low cost base. Their positions grew from – "Unconventional thinking, an ability to adapt to life-threatening crises, a global mind-set and disciplined ambition...crucial ingredients for achieving world-class status"[2].

Samsung, for example, moved out of the business of being simply a product provider and became a developer and marketer of brands. Brands, their intellectual property, and the relationships customers have with them, require sensitive security custodianship.

An Asian-founded global business competes not just on cost, but also on quality and innovation. One such operator innovates in small electric wine cellars and mini-fridges. In this organisation it is mandatory for employees to conceive of innovative ideas and insights. In an excellent analysis of these emerging markets, a former Dutch army officer who set up a specialist company dealing with emerging markets, goes on to give us more insights into emerging market companies, many that will become more prevalent in the future.

One such is a major electronics contract manufacturer, working with companies like Sony, Dell, Apple, IBM and Nokia. The company needs to manage chip design and other intellectual property from these competing customers. It needs to be discreet and also deliver world class manufacturing capability.

A shoe manufacturer, grown enormous, also finds maintaining and protecting differentiating brand properties is one of their greatest challenges as well as a critical success factor. Their security approach assures the prevention of leakage of intellectual property between brands. Where global brands unsurprisingly hold or should hold their suppliers responsible through rigid codes of conduct, manufacturers are getting increasingly closer to research, design and development, not simply the manufacture of goods, in line with the brand owners, through dedicated facilities. The drive to becoming innovators, not just imitators, is paramount. While the creation of new intellectual property remains dominated today by the established world, emerging markets are growing every day.

Way back in the 1980s, a Taiwanese semiconductor manufacturing company was struggling to get anyone to accept the viability of its vision. This vision was to be a dedicated integrated circuit foundry, or 'fab-maker', leaving the design and branding of chips to others. At that time, chip designers and chip designs were so proprietary that good designers were paranoid that irreplaceable intellectual property could be misused by selfish fabricators.

These kinds of organisations live or die by virtue of the quality of their corporate security approach and culture. A brand has no value if it cannot be trusted. Security systems that earn respect and confer confidence support values that can make or break a business.

Today, well over 50% of the designs of new models of wireless hand-helds, are by Taiwanese and other Asian companies. These successes came from breaking down barriers and prejudices. Success comes from the creation and execution of competitive intellectual property. Sustained success comes from the embedding of secure intellectual property in the operating culture.

Value is also in the minds of the people who work in these enterprises. Much of the information and intelligence that is important for business development is intangible, like the expression on a customer's face, or the mood in a factory, or the tone of voice of a government official. An intelligence-influenced approach to corporate security can play a key role in capturing this value.

In many ways, this approach can be distilled down to a three step process, which anyone can carry around in their head every day:

- What do we need to know?
- Where do we get it from?
- How do we use it profitably?

Visually this can be translated into an intelligence-influenced format that might look like this, and that can have several names and functions:

"Securing Value"

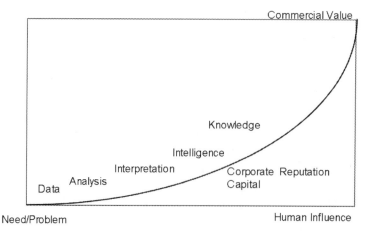

A Mexican-founded company is one of the world's largest cement makers. It is more profitable than its competitors and is a benchmark in efficiency. It believes commodities can benefit from branding. It has moved to the far right of the 'Securing Value' diagram. If cement can benefit from secure branding, what are we waiting for?

It is difficult to build a lasting business if there is little respect for the trading parties.[3] Where one tries to get the best deal out of another and they are doing the same back, or where as much risk as possible is passed to the other guy, progress will suffer. The real challenge most people face isn't about the quantity of information available, or about myopic perspectives, it's about *resistance to change despite qualified information*.

Security can play a significant role in managing this insight successfully.

One of the keys to this is in how people are treated for sharing or holding on to what they know. This is often about behaviour, culture, and politics more than about technology. Corporate security has a key contribution to make in determining management's approach to these critical strategic factors.

The idea of a secure social network within a corporate culture is critical to the idea of stimulating fresh intellectual property knowledge and creating learning. The extra challenge here is that since this is intangible, it is often ignored by management when decisions are taken on actions or investments to improve the way the business learns and shares knowledge within its own walls.

The last challenge is to start to think of secure networking knowledge as a brand value.

Brands can be partly assessed by the level of trust they can earn and the security they can confer. Brands are about the quality of the relationships they can engender. Many people aren't aware of the value of what they know. The loudest shouters aren't always the ones with the most valuable knowledge. People can't generally be forced into sharing knowledge, but corporate security can help the introduction of an acceptable secure social network approach.

"The key to success in the future of modern global companies will be in their ability to *create a corporate culture where people feel comfortable sharing experiences*." There are lessons we can take from all over the world. We all need to be prepared to change perspective. We need to be prepared to take action, and learn from others whoare already doing it.

Added value comes to secure sharers.

This is not a concept that sits naturally or comfortably in quite a number of people's corporate or business minds. Yet it is increasingly a method and an idea that is differentiating the best players from the rest. Unfortunately the same holds true for the criminally-minded, and certainly, the sharing of spoils and methods is working and has been embraced by major operators in illicit and illegal goods. Let us visit these parallel worlds and see how they co-exist with us.

> ***Security is a significant area of unrealised incremental value today.***
>
> ***Added value comes to secure sharers.***

2. Corruption and Closed Minds

"Gucci's Kelly Bag, which cost around 14000 euros, took 17 hours to produce – two hours more than the average car."[1] Copies are produced at a significantly less work-intensive rate.

"In Korea, one banker was asked by an investor to fax his proposal for a structured financial product directly to a competitor. The investor wanted a price from the competitor". Discretion was simply a waste of time"[2]

People should not be denied access to quality products and services, wherever they are. Yet there remain challenges around the globe as cultures and communities hold different ideas and expectations about value, originality, authenticity, and transparency. Security can play a significant role in supporting debate and action in what will continue to be a major consumer of time, money, and effort in determining acceptable parameters for intellectual property, rights, and values.

The CEO of a country operation for a major video and games company was driving along in his neighbourhood one Saturday morning. He was obliged to slow down suddenly on a narrow road, and drive onto the grass verge. A large van was trying to come through the other way. Helping it were two policemen on motorcycles, who stopped all other traffic and proceeded to direct the van driver to reverse into a narrower lane leading into a large field where many other vans, cars, and stalls were being set up. It was the Saturday morning 'car-boot sale' which was growing into a more standard kind of market. People turned up in thousands in search of bargains. The van was safely guided in, and the police sat waiting for the next challenge. The CEO decided to take a look for himself at the mobile market, and having got back on the road, he drove on a little way to the signs for a car park and moved into a space. There were plenty of stalls coming to life now, and as he walked past the large van he'd just witnessed being helped by the police, the rear doors opened wide. From front to back it was full of CDs and DVDs. As the CEO got closer, and watched the lads unloading the goods, he could see the titles of movies and games he hadn't yet got in his own outlets, all neatly packaged and priced, ready for eager punters looking to have the latest media offering at a bargain price. Not one piece of merchandise was official, and the buyers didn't care as long as the quality was good. Neither did the police.

The counterfeiting of film products costs the movie industry billions of dollars a year, a cost an eager public is unaware of, and can't relate to. Whatever the percentages and numbers industry monitoring companies produce to try and illustrate the actual amounts involved in all this activity, a totally accurate number is less useful than an appreciation of the enormous scale of the activity.

- In another example, after an 18 month operation, of careful investigation, surveillance, arrest, evidence collation, charging, trial, and conviction, a man, just one, who had been directly linked with the illicit copying, distribution and selling of DVDs, having some 20,000 copies of films in his possession, along with the machinery to copy them on premises registered to him, was fined a paltry amount, all the authorities could muster. By way of demonstrating his remorse, after the fine was announced, he asked the judge if he could have his 'stock' back, and the machinery that copied it. It was immediately returned

- Back in 2006, the Business Software Alliance Report announced an estimated $35 billion cost to the industry of counterfeited or illegally copied software. It was almost pleased to see that counterfeit levels in China had fallen from 92% to only 86% over a two year period – progress indeed.

- A factory in China was targeted and closed. It was estimated that the facility was producing over 50% of the copies of Gucci and Prada-type bags on sale in the New York area alone.

Despite stories like these, operators looking to work in places like China regard what they call 'the occasional bit of piracy' as the price of access to so lucrative a market. They say "What is the point here? It is time consuming, costly, and ineffective to sue those who copy us, and meanwhile our sales grow by 50–70% a year."[3] These circumstances have not stopped 800 German companies from registering with the German Chamber of Commerce in Shanghai, making it the largest organisation of its kind in the city and the largest outside Germany. For many of them, China represents less than 5% of their global sales today, but that could treble in ten years, so they just ask themselves, "Can you afford not to be here?"

This may be tolerable in a market, or markets, where intellectual property theft remains a major challenge – for a while. We would propose that integrated business security can help reduce pressures in a number of these extremely draining areas.

Before we look at this in depth, let's just capture another dimension. We noted earlier that value increasingly lies in intangibles. These days, that can be as much about impression and image as anything else. Just look at the list of the 'brands' remembered most by consumers from an International Survey[4] –

Apple	Google
Starbucks	Pixar
Amazon	Donald Trump
Martha Stewart	Oprah Winfrey

Two things are interesting here. First of all the number of people and services as opposed to classical branded goods like cars or jeans, and secondly note how many of these brands didn't have a real presence at all 20 years ago. iPod, eBay and Charles Schwab were also on the list. Brand has been redefined to embrace people and services whose 'trusted value' quotient is high. Of course, time creates change, and certainly in the eyes of the Inland Revenue Sercice, Martha Stewart didn't quite add up to their view of a trusted brand, and Donald Trump's position has also floated up and down over the years.

Even within the branded goods sector, there are new elements of value, which need to be protected, and which form the basis of further enabling value. "When you buy a Dell laptop, what are you buying? You are buying the guarantee of a rigorously managed supply chain. The brand is a triumph of quality and logistics. Each year's models are completely different from the last, but brand Dell provides the DNA."[5] But all of this talk of intangible value is just intellectual hot air, isn't it?

Look at how complex it really can get.

For those in the know, they have noticed that a factory producing Burberry raincoats for Burberry is also producing even better quality Burberry raincoats for the black market. Purchasers want the superior quality fake at a cheaper price. Not all fakes are inferior in the quality arena. Of course, in an Asian culture, copies are often regarded as an improvement on an original, in art as well as manufacturing. Copies become originals in their own right. The Western negative connotations of the dilution of an idea or quality don't exist in the same way. In the West, Burberry designs were adopted by a group of young people who used them as part of their cohort identity. This transient set was called Chavs by the people watchers and press. Burberry management were concerned at the potential deleterious effect this adoption of their branded clothes would have on their wider established market. So everyday brands can get sudden huge boosts or declines as organisations adapt them[6] and others simultaneously abandon them, from Doc Martens to Hush Puppies, from Slimfast to the Atkins Diet, from Barbour jackets to Belstaff. All have their time and place in the sun.

The challenge facing the brand managers is not simply one of capitalising on identified marketing opportunities, or responding to threats about diluting or substituted user bases, but about how to secure an evolutionary path to growth through these and other as yet unidentified adoptions.

Traditionally you might have expected to call in security to help you seize contraband, but would you seek security's view on helping you enable the business to manage and take advantage of these kinds of developments? Not often, so far. But not involving intelligence-influenced security can lead to very surprising problems for pressured marketing departments:

- In a routine investigation by the Japanese electronic company NEC into reports of fake equipment bearing its name, it emerged that an organised crime gang had effectively cloned the company and set up a parallel trading universe under the NEC name, with its own products, manufacturers and distribution network. Over 18 factories and 50 different products were involved in China and Taiwan. The real NEC was receiving customer complaints about products it did not make or supply with warranties.

- An army of Vietnamese workers in the Czech Republic, controlled by a mafia, were into a cigarette production operation. Production machinery and storage facilities were randomly moved or changed. At one small production centre it was estimated that 800 small trucks would have been necessary to move the finished product.

There is a growing scale and sophistication of counterfeiting operations, and close cooperation between and over borders is more and more necessary to deal with these kinds of operations.[7] "It is only through united efforts by both the public and private sectors that real success in combating counterfeiting and piracy can be achieved", said Interpol's Secretary General Ronald Noble.[8]

For international operations you need international solutions and shared leadership. Business needs to conjoin with intelligence, and move from understanding to operations. Leading businesses, the World Intellectual Property Organisation, INTERPOL, World Customs, and the International Chambers of Commerce have now had annual congresses and regional gatherings, fostering this view.

The perception of value is being made more complex in markets like the fashion world, which regularly like to shake up norms. There is a company in London that has a branded operation called Fake. Anti-counterfeit operators need to achieve sophisticated levels of understanding of marketing developments, so they can acquire a better capability to conduct operations against serious organised crime. An example is business co-operating to facilitate an Interpol operation[9] co-ordinating the activities of three national law enforcement agencies to deal with counterfeiting in the region bordered by Argentina, Brasil, and Paraguay.

But it seems like anyone can get on the counterfeit trail.

The driver is profit, which can be as powerful a motivator as God[10].

"Criminal networks thrive on international mobility and the ability to take advantage of the opportunities that flow from the separation of marketplaces into sovereign states with borders. For criminals, frontiers create business opportunities and convenient shields."

As organised crime syndicates grow, they begin to look like corporations themselves, and the smarter of those realise that this leads to a slowdown in nimbleness. Networks, neural links, cells, become much more effective by working and keeping ahead of the legal chasers. In fact some countries now operate like this, especially those where the criminal networks are often also the most powerful political players. It is difficult for the mastodons of bureaucratic democracy to contain these evolving entities.

In Afghanistan, a policeman might get $300 pay a month, if he gets paid at all. That's not exactly a high barrier to entry for enterprising criminals to establish friendly relations with the 'force' of law. Governments can't match the economic motives of brand owners and copiers in many markets, but lessons and experiences can often be transferred from one example to another. We return again to the theme of sharing and efficiency.

Improving interagency collaboration between, say, anti-illicit trade (AIT) specialists and others who have valuable information and resources is more and more necessary, but it takes more than simply re-organising reporting lines. There needs to be a synchronising of the roles and behaviours of the involved agencies. Seizing goods is maybe good for PR, but not good as a strategic weapon against the heart of illicit operations. Too many people are tied up in after-the-horse-has-bolted remits, and don't have the skills to cut off AIT at its roots.

The traditional approach was always a "leave it to the lawyers" one, which can be great where the law is effective, as in some developed markets. But it often doesn't make sense in emerging markets, so the challenge becomes "What can be done where the law is not enough yet?"

Once you get away from traditional thinking, you can embrace new thinking. This means you don't pursue a purely law driven approach, and instead start to examine the full nature of counterfeiting activity by organised crime and ways to tackle it. Here the focus shifts from infraction of the law out to the full spectrum of activity that gets a product from inception right through to the market place, and 'interfering' with that process. This requires intelligence, and the mechanisms to acquire and process it. Such intelligence should cover product sourcing, manufacture, packaging, warehousing and distribution, sales and customer feedback. This often requires informant protection, which is second nature for intelligence and security agencies, and the ability of businesses to engage with public security and law enforcement agencies.

This is the best way to ensure that intelligence assessments are delivered in a timely and efficient manner to ensure that appropriate enforcement actions can be taken. These actions do not simply involve taking criminals to court. They involve the seizure and destruction of product, the closing down of factories and manufacturing plant. It is also necessary to ensure the responsible activity of legitimate suppliers to avoid their inadvertently supporting illegal production.

This broadening of the process of countering the counterfeiters beyond the single function of, say, the law officers, into a process of multifunction ownership and action has been successfully created by different perceptions and players being brought to the table by security, and the leveraging influence of the assembled organisations on corrupt politicians and governments.

Overall, counterfeiters are estimated to sell up to £10 billion of fake goods a year in Britain alone,[11] from sportswear and cigarettes to perfume and medicines, from DVDs to compact discs. Not long ago, counterfeit Lipton teabags made up 67% of foodstuffs seized. Adidas and Nike copies accounted for 27% and 26% of seized sportswear. L'Oreal reported that in a three year period its activity to seize counterfeit products increased at an annual rate of 30%, and so did its expenses.

Let us go to the next stage of looking at corruption and closed minds.

"It wasn't long before the politics of intelligence undermined everything Dewey tried to do."[12]

"The secret of life is honesty and fair dealing; if you can fake that you've got it made."[13]

Professional corporate security management should play a core role in building the links between the way a company or organisation does its business, the quality and the depth of its relationships with the community, and its ability to operate in a safe and sustainable way.

In a poll conducted in the heady pre-recession days of August 2005,[14] 72% of respondents felt wrong-doing was widespread in all industries, up from 66% just a year earlier. And just 2% thought CEOs of large companies to be "very trustworthy". Consumers have wised up to the way corporations behave and are using trust, or lack of it, as a guide to purchasing choices more than before. But this has often come at a horrendous cost.

Hubris and incompetence are not an endearing combination. Linked to corruption they create a fatal triad. This example was used to demonstrate that this triad of elements permeated the interpretation of the intelligence gathering process to promote war in Iraq in 2003[15]. Similar behaviour emanated from the top of the World Bank, in the form of its president, who was particularly public about the crusade to stay clear of corruption, yet tried to hang on to his role after deliberately trying to secure promotion and 'above pay-grade' compensation in the bank for his girlfriend. Eliot Spitzer followed suit in New York. In the face of this kind of behaviour, any campaign for good governance is seen as "not a believable struggle, but blatant hypocrisy".

In other cases people regularly turn a blind eye, or eyes, to unpalatable truths, because they think so-and-so is a 'regular guy', or because they feel they are in a privileged position and can come to no harm. An even cursory look at the auditing set-up of one organisation should have raised eyebrows, and did, but this emperor's new clothes advice was ignored in the pursuit of what appeared to be failsafe huge gains. This was what Bernard Madoff brought to the party in 2008, a fraud still being estimated that affected a large number of enterprises, let alone individuals, who should have known better but chose to ignore what was there to see right in front of them.

It is obvious that decisions are rarely based on facts alone – the role of emotions and instincts in influencing the decision-making process cannot be underestimated. "How many decisions, including ones of great historical significance that impact millions of people, are made by men and women who are driven by personal motives rather than by a desire to do the right thing?"[16]

On a grander scale,[17] "many perceive governments getting weaker in the context of a global economy run by corporations in the interests of their own profit, not by politics in the interests of their own people". Values are no longer provided by states alone, and the descriptor, 'statesman', has not been used in glowing terms for some time. Other commentators note that[18] what may be self-evident and compulsory in our view of business ethics very likely appears cloudy and innocuous from the perspectives of many others. Corruption is an elusive creature, and presents particular risks for security and its paymasters.

An anonymous report of a fraud by a finance manager was received in one of the countries of the former central republic of the USSR's office of a global company. After investigation, it was discovered that actually three people had been defrauding the company. Having obtained the evidence, the case was handed over to the local police who prosecuted it. The principal offender was sentenced to 18 years hard labour and the other two got 15 years hard labour each. On appeal the 18 year sentence was reduced to 15 and the 15 year sentences to 12. The defrauded sum was in the area of $4 million.

Initial feelings were of euphoria. Then the second thoughts came through. What were the chances of these people serving out their time in hard labour in a country of that sort? How does it fit with any Western-based sense of balance of punishment, human rights, and reputation? Could the company be accused of being responsible for what might amount to 'a death sentence'?

Companies are held to account for the impact they have on these issues in their home jurisdictions all the time. This approach shows the danger of following a simple criminal process without considering the broader ramifications and the potential effect on damage to the company from any number of stakeholders.

In another organisation, the CSO discovered at a regional meeting that in one country the use of lie detectors was routine when conducting any investigations. This would not have been condoned in the company's home jurisdiction at all. The question of human rights becomes more complex on a global stage, with companies coming to market from many different perspectives and starting points.

High performance makes demands on everyone. Mature managers know that employees at all levels face temptations. Unconstrained, these pressures produce corrupt capitalism. The Chief Legal Officer at General Electric[19] observed that there has to be a policy to fuse high performance with high integrity. Lapses in integrity can have catastrophic effects on companies. A policy then needs to become part of an 'integrity culture'. Implementing global standards of best practice can create a strong reputation for integrity that will complement and enhance the company.

Corruption and its interpretation, then, are not absolutes, but conditional elements, growing as a leitmotif of the 21st century. It is all embracing. There is corruption that is personal risk and corruption that is political risk, global risk or local community risk. Political risk, especially where corruption provides the mantra for the modus operandi, significantly affects business environments and is a threat to core company values and the ability to conduct business, except of course in those companies that share the values of the controlling political organisation. A civil war impacts on everything, and a decision to nationalise an industry has specific and focused consequences. Companies clearly also vary in scale, ambition and impact, and it is necessary to be able to judge the extent to which they have the desire and drive to be politically active. This has a major effect on the extent to which they expose themselves to reputation damage in the face of political change. Some would argue that reputation risk is intangible and hard to measure, but it is clear to others that businesses can suffer significant losses – money, trust, and lives once reputation has been damaged through allegations of corruption.

Risk assessment models and quality intelligence sources can help people get a better grip on emerging scenarios of corruption threats in countries and regions, and help them plan for action as various outcomes and developments are projected.

Key to security's contribution in this arena is an ability to draw constructive conclusions about what outcomes might emerge from the interconnectivity of relationships between governments, their national constituents, and business. It is not enough to know about the implications of change from taxation or regulations, but it is critical to be able to supply informed views based on a close understanding of the people involved in critical developments and decisions, which cannot yet be delegated to software programmes.

Professional security management should play a core role in forging the links between the ways a company or organisation does its business, the quality and the depth of its relationships with the community, and its ability to operate in a safe and sustainable way.[20]

Yet to survive in this environment, the challenged security team also needs to appreciate two further key elements, captured in the quotes and perspectives of two managers:

- "There is no point trying to be the most secure company in the world. We need to be the most successful company."
- "Chief executives don't want a security manager who constantly tells them what they *can't* do. They want people who will help them to push the boundaries without *unduly* compromising the company".

General Electric encourages finance, legal and HR to be both partners and guardians. They are a crucial part of the corporation's basic checks and balances. "But these functions cannot be effective unless they are also deeply involved in helping to develop and execute commercial strategies. Leaders need to assume the dual role of partner and guardian, and manage the tension between them."[21]

In a world of unceasing corruption, the emerging security professional needs to be very clear what *unduly* means. Unduly is one of those words lawyers love. Get the best opinion you can. This is called 'opinion shopping'. Match the most suitable opinion to the lawyer with the biggest clout and you'll probably be saving yourself a lot of hassle. Similarly, a view needs to formed, objectively, that helps identify the extent to which the respected security professional can contribute, should, or not, in special kinds of operations, like in the following scenario:

"The narcissistic organisation becomes a moral universe of its own, a world where its goals, goodness and means are not questioned but taken as a holy writ. It's a world where doing whatever we need to, to get whatever we want, seems perfectly fine. The on-going celebration fogs over how divorced from reality we've become. The rules don't apply to us, just to the others."[22]

Corruption isn't going to go away quietly. One US security consultant in London was paid more than the director of the CIA and the President of the US put together. She had an open first class ticket to fly back and forward to the US any time. In London she rented some of the priciest office space available. When the CIA went out to inspect, they found she had subleased the office, defrauding the government. The woman who had set up the payment to the London consultant resigned from the CIA on a Friday and went to work for the same company the London-based woman worked for the following Monday.

As an ex CIA operative summarised it, "The mantra at 1600 Pennsylvania Avenue seemed to be: get through the term. Keep the bad news from the newspapers. Dump the naysayers. Gather money for the next election, lots and lots of it, and let some other administration down the line deal with it all."[23]

Institutionalised corruption becomes well disguised as professional business practice. In financial markets, one of the first examples of this was the introduction of 'swaps' into an over-the-counter market (OTC). Major banks suddenly took centre stage, and became strong advocates of OTC derivatives markets and marketing. Not only could large amounts of money be made, there was a significant and convenient absence of transparency in the OTC market. This was a world where dealers dealt with each other or their clients, and information about the specifics of trades and prices was consciously suppressed, suiting the dealers just fine. In fact they ensured that clients didn't know the true price of what was being traded. You were not subject to the same rules as those dealing through exchanges.

The perpetual push to avoid transparency and maximise profit has defined the derivatives markets ever since. This is at the heart of derivatives profitability.[24] Transparency was, and is considered to be, the providence of fools, although electronic trading has curtailed a lot of that, and taken the 'fun' out of the business for many now rich retired players. Ethical debates have never featured highly with some of the 'big swinging dicks'. Dealers make money, lots of it. Risk managers, compliance, legal, accounting, operations, security – they're just costs. If the tension between the two could be harvested for energy the world would run green for some time. Dealers don't listen (to you) and don't trust anyone. If you can get them to derivatise security then maybe you and they will make great friends and a lot of money – for a while. People who have put their faith in a conveniently Gaussian world of predictable distribution curves don't want to know about 'chaos' and 'power law distribution', unless they can make even more money out of them. Sadly, the same people[25] forget or never knew that the idolised Gauss originally intended the 'normal distribution' model as a test of error, not accuracy.

Paul Valery, a bit like Yogi Berra, said that "the future is like everything else, it is not what it was."[26] The past does not always repeat itself, except in one fundamentally human way. There are always plenty of people around who think they can get rich following the pronouncements and practices of a few wise men, or readers of entrails. These days we call these people fund managers and quantitative analysts. Increased risk management systems seem to do little to reduce the losses these financial giants are capable of generating from time to time. You don't know when the next hit is going to occur. That's it. You also don't know what losses risk management has saved you from. It's back to the world of known unknowns.

Another story reveals how the National Australia Bank in 2004 lost around $360 million in trading foreign exchange options. The bank's board recognised risk was important but didn't seem too concerned about the practicalities of it – the audit committee was lost in process, and the risk committee met infrequently and didn't look at breaches of VAR (Value at Risk) risk limits. After the independent inquiry presented its findings the board engaged in a war of mutual accusation, and the head of risk had already been ousted.

We know that financial institutions, by and large, need to take 'risks' to make money, but risk management is becoming a toothless dog, or scapegoat, for excesses. In a world where ever more complex, almost atomically detailed investment products are created by quantum physicist educated modellers, Heisenberg's Uncertainty Principle seems to kick in to confirm that you really can't know everything that's going on. The real world isn't interested in conforming to assumptive models. The real world is much wackier than that.

There was a company that decided to move out of a capital city to be nearer its predominantly green-field clients and demonstrate its commitment to being on hand to service their needs. They promptly lost much of their business. They hadn't worked out that many of their clients chose them because they were in the capital, and because it gave them an excuse to be out of the office occasionally and having a good time.

One corporate treasurer's only concern when dealing with an investment bank was, "Will I still get an invitation to the bank's box for the finals of the US Tennis Open if a junior salesperson covers my business?"

Robert Citron, the treasurer of Orange Country, California, managed to have his name attached to the loss of more than $1.5 billion through derivative trading on the behalf of his unknowing flock. He was sure there was no risk when things were going well. "I am one of the largest investors in America. I know these things", he said in July 1993. On December 6, 1994, Orange County filed for bankruptcy. The court proceedings unveiled Citron's investment strategy. He relied on the advice of a psychic and a mail order astrologer for financial guidance, using a $4.50 chart prepared by an Indianapolis star-reader to help manage Orange County's money.

Country leaders have also been prone to using such guidance. The learning is that there are always plenty of people around who want to be led to fortune – and then fall into its downside, disaster. This is apparent from a social pathology insight – psychopaths rally followers.

If you want to add value as a security professional in environments like this, you need to be very sure what value means in those specific contexts. If you're not deep-in-the-money, you're going to find fulfilment a challenge. On the other hand, keeping these kinds of folks out of jail may be stimulation of a different order.

Finally, we will stretch our minds a little further on the subject of closed minds, and what we need to do to open them:

- We must plan for freedom, and not only for security, if for no other reason than that only freedom can make security secure.
- Falsifiable theories enhance our control over error while expanding the richness of what we can say about the world.

Citing the philosopher Karl Popper[27] to support security's mission may seem to be stretching a point, but he gave time brilliantly to analysing the way of the world for us to build on.

Modern security is the business of rationalising paradoxes, pragmatically.

If someone says to you, "We don't have any problems. We know what we're doing", you can surmise at least six things:

1. They don't have any problems. They know what they're doing.

2. They don't have any problems, but they don't know what they're doing.

3. They may have problems, and they're working on it.

4. They may have problems and they're not working on it.

5. They may have problems. They just don't know it.

6. You're not the one they're going to tell, whatever.

After the Challenger space shuttle exploded on January 28, 1986, a committee of inquiry was established. It was told – there was a big problem, there would be a least a year for the inquiry, lots of people will be crawling all over it.The late Professor Richard Feynman, one of the 20th century's leading theoretical physicists, with a penchant for reducing things to a graspable level, was one of those invited on to the inquiry. He listened to the briefing about the tragedy and had a hunch, which took him to Florida and the launch site. Six weeks later, having talked to a lot of people on the ground at Cape Canaveral, he knew what had happened. He demonstrated to the inquiry what had happened on that fateful day in a way that high-school kids could immediately grasp. It was all about cold temperatures and shrinking O-rings, basic physics. One of the most vociferous complaints from the committee was that Feynman had cracked the issue with some 46 weeks of inquiry left to run, and that was really spoiling the party for a number of the members. How insensitive of Feynman.

Closed minds produce different perspectives:

- "Guitar-based bands are over." D Rowe, Head of Decca Records, on turning down the Beatles for a record contract.

- "I don't see why anyone would ever want more than 64k of computing power at home. " W (Bill) Gates.

- "Peace in our time". Neville Chamberlain.

"Can new security architectures meet the challenges of the 21st century?" Charlie Edwards of the think-tank, Demos asked.The short answer is – not without further work. The general problem we face is that in many circumstances new structures are not even fully of the 20th century, let alone the 21st, especially in the West. Principles practised in empire management times continue to have a legacy effect.

The foundations of many government operations are based on fading heydays. The last but one time when dramatic change was needed to meet new events was the collapse of the Soviet Union. This meant a new shift in the notion of 'balancing powers'. We are waiting for a fresh period of balance. As John Darwin[28] notes, empire lives on. We are simply trying to analyse who will have the next one. We also have a more global economy than ever, which is a key driver of politics, and whose combination of success and anarchy placed us in an interesting period of tension. President Obama, amongst others, is now trying to effect dramatic change in the face of the newest set of dramatic events. With these tectonic shifts it is interesting to see that governments, organisations and even entrepreneurial operations still organise themselves into departments. Departments are structures like castles, built to keep people out but ultimately trapping their own people within in a myopic form of defence.

We have departments like we had castles because they are an evolutionary form. We are comfortable with them in a way we are not comfortable with dramatic change. In a microscopic UK example, see how long it took the Serious Organised Crime Agency (SOCA) to evolve. Its evolution cannot be described as a shining example of the survival of the fittest. Post-heyday life remains all about edging forward. Development happens not because of a lack of brain power, but because of the inertial weight of vested interests protecting status quos.

Departments become institutionalised, like their controlling institutions, and are defended at all costs, as are the careers of their gatekeepers. This is coupled with loyalty to career creators and peer organisations. Changes, naturally, are perceived threats. This serves to reinforce step-by-step approaches e.g. "We'll get there in the end". This is probably not the best way to deal with emerging major threats and events, whose structures and behaviours have evolved differently.

One of the problems is that the starting point for too many is "What shall we do in the department to meet these threats?" as opposed to asking the more fundamental questions like "What is the situation we face today?" and "How are we best able to manage this?" With answers to these questions it may then be wise to tackle how the best structure might be utilised to handle the emerging scenario.

Not enough people are asking the macro questions, or, if they are, being listened to.

- How do you secure national interests in the modern world?
- What capabilities are needed? These may not even exist, so don't go looking for them in a department designed to do something different.

Pre SOCA the view was that of course everyone could cooperate and collaborate if they wanted to, but the reality in the UK was that the 43 or so police forces couldn't really talk to each other in depth. They had different capabilities, their computer systems were incompatible, and they were trained differently. As an American observer might summarise it, "They claimed to sleep in the same bed but they all had different dreams". This is the kind of place many corporations found themselves in during the 1960s. Those that recognised it and were highly competent did something about it and survive today, heartily. Too many enterprises seem to want to thrive on a form of fossilisation, presuming history will finally bestow some form of retrospective accord upon them.

Maybe there should be an Agency for National Interest (not a department!) in countries, which suggests this should be an enveloping and embracing entity, but definitely not a smothering one. Whatever, there needs to be something flexible and able which is more substantially effective than a statement of cooperation.

What further resources are needed? Usually everyone rushes to demand extra or new resources that are often not required, which we will illustrate later. These can hinder progress where those same extra bodies take up the time of experienced predecessors or practitioners who have to train the newcomers in new skills. 'Body-building' is also a costly exercise and certainly not the most affordable solution beyond certain levels. Combining skills and knowledge may be more productive than simply raising headcounts.

Again the early question should be about identifying what needs to be done, and then to look at how to structure the resource to fulfil that. In a modern world, like in the commercial sphere, it is harder and harder to separate the home market from the international market. In the same way, national, or home security, is harder to separate from international security. We all have far more links and connectivity, dependencies, on international things than ever before. In this context it is both surprising and alarming to note that the UK's Critical National Infrastructure strategy doesn't even feature financial services, but it is just possible that this year someone may be reconsidering that.

Some things need to be more joined together, once they have been introduced at the party. For instance, in this context, joining security and intelligence forces, and not seeing them as essentially different, should be a productive development. In the UK, MI5 and MI6 would find this to be anathema, because their institutionalised cultures would force them to continue predominantly to only see differences, not synergies.

Organisations develop a persona, a culture, over time, which, as they mature, like people, makes them different from others – recognisable but different. These differences become embodiments of the culture, and the living organisation then seeks to recruit and develop personalities or offspring that best reflect these embodiments. When you sit down with people from these different organisations you quickly spot the way they adopt and reflect the cultures they are in. What they embody, and what they want to preserve, is almost part of a brand – Brand MI5 or Brand The Metropolitan Police Force, or Brand The Judiciary, and Brand The Civil Service. People defending these cultures, and their 'brand values', say that's what gives them their strength – their differentiation, their core values. This in turn drives their core loyalty. For anything new to succeed, its newness has to eventually become embedded and embodied. All too often this takes longer than the threat it was designed to combat, which has evolved to another form or level. This is what so often slows down or destroys merger and acquisition programmes in commercial enterprises. Intangibles are not sufficiently factored in to the drive to achieve 'numerical' added values. This is why successful Brand Management is a real skill, and why a number of brands do not enjoy long and prosperous lives.

In any National Interest Agency or function, there would also need to be a strong representation of commerce, partly because it is business which appears to be able to respond to the need for rapid change – the 'profit imperative', even if it doesn't always get things right first time around, and partly because it is increasingly difficult to separate nation states and needs from corporations and needs. Also, on a boringly pragmatic and embarrassing note, if you don't engage commerce, you don't have any funding for all the other things you need.

On this basis, we would argue that there is as much a need for a Business Security Collection Plan as any other plan in a global economic environment. Coordination between business and state is happening, but vested interests still mean that things don't happen smoothly, and there are constant friction points. There is no point edging towards being ready for something that should have been present from the outset. The mentality is too much about "Well, how do we shuffle?" towards where we are meant to be going. At that speed even the destination can get lost in the distance and time passed.

Of course, another thing that comes along with institutions is pride, and not far behind that can come a sense of patronisation. "Why do those folk outside this institution need to know that?" is the attitude, and information remains the currency of power for these people. But the jaw-dropper here is that governments need to be more open on security issues. "It's not good for the public to know that" needs to be handled very carefully in an elected democratic political environment.

There are significant issues of ethics and governance related to openness and transparency. Where there is no openness there is usually questionable activity and possible corruption. Government should be subject to goals on openness in the ways companies like Transparency International advocate for business. Businesses are being driven to being more open on issues like corporate social responsibility, versus their previous behaviour that was often hidden behind walls of deniability. This is more than saying "Yes but we already have a Freedom of Information Act", which is a relative issue versus other issuances, as in the US. With openness comes a different form of responsibility that is mature enough to admit that embarrassment about failures should not precondition negative attitudes to confidentiality, distortion, secrecy or repression.

This openness should also mean that the electorate itself, yes, the people, can play a greater part in contributing to the security of their domain. To be more open you need more accountability, but those responsible for accountability need to have more power. The questions then move to a new plain.

Does having an open and accountable entity enable organisations to function more freely and successfully? Evidence we have used in this book from emerging markets alone would suggest that this is a sound and valuable strategy to pursue. Does moving in this direction allow us all to benefit from better economic and political relations with others abroad, and to work in an unthreatening manner? Just like in a successful business, country 'plc' shareholders, the electorate, need to know they are receiving value from their elected investment, and they are entitled to seeing both quantitative and qualitative appraisals of that value-generating role and contribution.

Saying "We can't measure this" means "We don't want to go there". This is an approach or attitude that is culturally and often also politically bound and needs to change. Measurement is possible, and is not simply a function of accounting.

There will always be unanticipated things that happen. Some would argue this is a *fault* of intelligence. It is becoming worrying that there has to be a blame element for all actions, a deliberate causality, not an accidental randomness. Human beings control everything, so they must be responsible for everything. At least that's the victim's argument. Some would argue that is why we must keep departments and forms of government consistent i.e. unchanged for as long as possible. Energy needs to be devoted to establishing the (human) cause of all things, shout the Health & Safety Brethren. Others would accept that the contribution of intelligence and open minds is more about helping those charged with managing the responses to unexpected events cope and handle situations better, without being thrown significantly off-track.

This is a difference of both perception and expectation.

A closed Indian economy, closed minds, closed borders, and a lack of communications, made it very difficult to move good ideas around the country quickly until the early 1990s. It had poor roads, red tape, congested ports, inflexible labour laws, corruption, and power outages. Apart from the roads, it sounds like California, except it was the opposite of a draw for both foreign and domestic investment. But free-market reforms changed all that. Today India produces over 100,000 highly qualified engineers every year, and many of them are no longer immediately rushing off to the US or Europe to get jobs. They are staying, in places like Bangalore. More people in Indian organisations believe in a corporate culture of transparency and meritocracy, and they stress the values of integrity and imagination. They have discovered that creating a global mind-set that seeks global benchmarking builds confidence, and that good corporate governance is a sign of integrity and often helps stock prices. Constant adaptation to changing circumstances is strategy in practice.

Professional corporate security management should play a core role in building the links between the way a company or organisation does its business, the quality and the depth of its relationships with the community, and its ability to operate in a safe and sustainable way.

Modern security is the business of rationalising paradoxes, pragmatically.

Ask yourself, next time you are faced with a challenge "What kind of response do we need, what kind of organisation is needed?" as opposed to "How are we going to preserve our organisation against this threat, or change?"

---

3. A Fresh Start – Outset Security

How can security be a valuable contributor and business enabler, without detriment to its expected role as a protective agent? We introduce the idea of how an outset security approach can support an organisation's full set of values including its reputation. Getting there requires certain changes in thinking and practice, which also means revising views and notions about the old established order, or historical world of security.

Once upon a time, corporate security was borne out of necessity, peopled with corporate cops and perimeter fences. This role is often now just a small but still important element of protection for leading integrated business security players. The new world is one where the idea of outset security becomes a corporate reflex, not a 'by invitation' service. Let's take a closer look at it.

Outset security is a set of operating conditions where security issues are addressed at the same time as all other key strategic or functional issues in an enterprise. As in the famous example of chaos theory – the butterfly flaps its wings in the Pacific, and there is a storm in Seattle three weeks later... small, simple changes in the initial conditions of a plan or enterprise can lead to enormous differences in outcomes. The absence of intelligence-influenced security at the outset of planning and execution will have a similarly profound effect on how things develop, turn out, and are perceived.

In this evolution, security can no longer be regarded like the Victorian child who was expected to be seen and not heard. We will show what happens when security is released from its vital but constrained protective role, and invited to play a 'consciously competent' role throughout an organisation's activities, culture, and cross-functional leadership.

Getting more value from security takes time and effort. There is no simple formula, no one set of metrics to be applied, just like there is no standard organisation or culture. What we do know is that shared approaches to releasing security's potential lead to surprising results, and worthwhile rewards.

People need to be prepared to revise views and positions on security's role and potential. For example, who gets recognition and high rewards for avoiding risk or preventing disasters, for valuing what we don't know? Logic suggests that for many distressing things it is better to have prevention than treatment, but few reward acts of prevention. If prevention can also be inextricably linked to demonstrable value, then medals can be cast and badges of success can be worn. Some corporate stars come to understand that while they remain in the spotlight, security has a backstage pass – access all areas. Some people know how valuable that can be.

We need to be prepared to be surprised some more.

To become more efficient, a Canadian logging company has implemented technology systems so that even before a tree is cut down the company knows whether it will be used for pulp or lumber, which mill will process it, which retailer will stock it, even the precise size of each piece of lumber that will come from it, and which building, home, or office it will be used to build. This saves money, eliminates waste, lowers transport costs, and makes everyone more profitable.[1]

Dell doesn't make a single computer until a customer has specified it and paid for it. These ways of working are about invention, innovation, iteration, and integration. They are what we also use to describe an approach to business-integrated security that is anticipatory and far-sighted. It doesn't mean the resultant organisation is predictive in a Tarot-card reading sense, but in the sense that anyone associating with such an approach is likely to be more prepared to respond productively to what might happen.

This approach requires adaptability and versatility. There is a need for specialists with deep skills and narrow focus in this approach, giving practitioners expertise that is ultimately recognised by peers. There is also a need for 'versatilists'[2] who apply a depth of skill to a progressively widening scope of situations, gaining 'new competencies, building relationships, and assuming new roles'.

In marketing departments, there used to be people who would go along and say to a researcher – "We need some research". This would usually contain the unspoken desire "... that will support my premeditated point of view". The wise researcher would say, "You may need some research, but before we get to that, tell me more about what you are trying to find out". Wise research is about discovery.

- "We need some security".
- "We need more security".
- "We don't need all this security".
- "No way are we paying for that".

These kinds of statements may often be delivered by senior managers with no reference to security people.

A CCTV system is installed at great expense, with the wrong kind of lenses for the task at hand. An M&A project is initiated by an ambitious director. Two thirds of the way through the project on a need to know basis, a token input from security is requested.

Security's seasoned response in the first case would have been to define the nature of the surveillance required before commissioning the fitment. In the second case, security due diligence would have revealed earlier that senior targets in the M&A project had questionable pasts and motivations which could seriously jeopardise the acquiring company's future reputation. There are embarrassing stand offs, and then an expensive but quiet withdrawal wrapped up in a tale of normal due diligence discovering conflicts of interest.

The strategic application of outset security would have saved time, money, reputation, and embarrassment. The point is, whether it is from the security leader or not, outset security questions should be an integrated element of any board driven actions. No commercial airplane captain would commence a flight without saying "Your safety is our primary concern".

Let's look at some examples of how outset security might have led to a different outcome. All these examples are real, with source data protected. It is necessary to remind ourselves that many organisations are reluctant to share their failures on a public stage, or even in some cases in a small private venue. There is little appetite for the Alcoholics Anonymous approach to confession. For this reason, where we can, we identify companies who have given permission for their triumphs and tragedies to be shared. Otherwise we have abstracted the examples, so that while the details are true, you can still benefit from others experience, albeit anonymously derived.

Often the CSO has to try to persuade other departments to carry out best practice, while those departments carry the burden of cost and effort, and are therefore reluctant to participate until faced with the consequences of ignoring the advice. A recurrent example of this is in the area of personnel recruitment, where a number of HR departments will assure you that they carry out screening of potential employees, while in reality they don't do it for specific specialised roles, or the screening is highly generalised. Perhaps the greatest losses to business are from internal fraud, often undisclosed. Where investigations are undertaken – not always – the true track record of the culprit, if it had been known previously, would have often led to his or her de-selection from employment. It is said that at least 25% of CVs contain falsehoods. A good approach is to identify a screening process for all recruits, with a graduated increase in inspection and specificity as the post becomes more vital to the company.

We are now living in a world that is flush with opportunity and greater risk, simultaneously. Financial markets try to benefit from this tension every day. In this environment, security's role should be to enable business to fulfil its objectives where inaction might itself be too risky. Security is the fulcrum on which are balanced the scales of opportunity and risk. The best security has a role to play in the interplay of entrepreneurs and risk managers. Where a senior banking manager fired a risk management specialist for pointing out the imminent danger of their company's over-exposure to risk, which subsequently happened, there is something profoundly wrong with the role and respect for security in the operating culture.

A particularly enlightened CEO used to give his fellow board members an annual opportunity to see for themselves just what the risk-reward equation meant in reality. One board meeting a year would be held in one of the organisation's more challenging environments, so that senior people could remind themselves, or be more acquainted with, the context in which their colleagues were working to support goals and objectives. Board members were helped to appreciate the steps that would be taken to provide their personal protection, and at the same time they were immersed in a market where they could clearly see that without world-class outset security in practice, there would be no business for them to be witnessing, and no revenue contribution to be celebrating.

So when the nervous board director asks, "Are we more secure than last year?" how can that be demonstrated? If the CEO isn't taking security as a personal agenda item, your company, its values, and its reputation, are at risk. It's probably time to state that the absolute leader of security in an organisation must be the CEO.

Since we are continuously talking about perspective, look at this in another way. Security takes care of clutter, so you are freed up to be more productive in other areas where you can identify, nurture, and deliver value. Or at least claim a big slice of it.

A new office was located for a multinational company wanting to expand its operations in the Middle East. Beirut was the preferred base. The security officer, aware of Beirut's past, judged that although the city was relatively quiet, and certainly more so than in previous decades, the possibility of renewed urban bombing activity could not be sensibly discounted. He therefore recommended that the new office building's windows be bomb-filmed as a precaution against such an eventuality. The regional business director rejected this proposal as adding too much to the cost of operations.The security officer, bravely or foolishly depending on your view of the prevailing operating culture, took his case to global security, and there the directors reviewed the case and agreed to support the investment proposal. Some months later, former President Hariri was killed by a bomb which caused widespread damage in the area immediately adjacent to the offices in question. This building was the only one whose windows were protected, saving upwards of 50 lives. The business was also up and running again within 20 hours. The relationship between the security officer and the business director was substantially improved. This intelligence influenced approach to outset security added immeasurably to the perceived value of the operation from the standpoint of its employees, and was a realistic investment. The director made sure his ultimate endorsement of the investment decision also did no lasting damage.

> ### *Security is no longer a side dish.*

4. Making Security a Competitive Asset

Security is a significant area of unrealised incremental value today.[1]

For global and multinational organisations, operational challenges have never been so demanding. The means to attack or destroy value have never been so cheap, deep and relentless. For specialists in security management, there will be a need to reinforce security's core role in the coming years, enhancing its ability to make a significant contribution as an integrated business function.

Try and imagine someone being held responsible for security or risk management getting rewarded as equally as a market maker. It may be hard to envisage that, and it isn't surprising that security is still only regarded as a passive protective agent in many market-making enterprises. But this is changing in enlightened environments.

For years, security was principally about barriers, about keeping things safe, about avoiding the consequences of unwanted attacks and intrusion. All well and good, and this role remains a vital pillar in the foundation of any strong successful business. But today there are also plenty of reasons to regard security as having the potential to fulfil a more pro-active role as an enabling tool, as a means of making a marked contribution to the performance, reputation and trust of an enterprise, wherever it operates.

In most companies, security management is not fully embedded as a commercial function and does not engage on equal terms with other core business functions. This is a performance and cultural issue. It is also a thought leadership issue.

In essence, security can make a significant contribution to increased shareholder value. Let's look at one scenario.

In one operation, organised crime gangs had made much out of attacks on the logistics supply chain of a business in Brasil. For non-residents, it is worth pointing out that Brasil is the size of Europe. Convoys were being attacked by machine-gun armed organisations and losses were running at over $50 million per year, despite the presence of escort services. However, escort services by law were not allowed to carry weapons that matched the type of arms used by the aggressors. The police and the army were reluctant to get involved at the time. The annual security budget to protect this activity was $200,000. The company was persuaded to invest in this aspect of security to the level of $2,000,000 per year. Funded operations were based on an intelligence-influenced process, satellite tracking facilities, covert as well as overt escort capability, and post-theft investigation processes. The promise given for the investment was that the losses would be reduced to at least one fifth of the previous levels. In the event losses thereafter never exceeded $1 million per year. The new security approach also led to the provision of evidence that enabled a now motivated police force to completely dismember a nationwide organised crime organisation. A figure of $1 million losses for $2 million spent looks a lot better when you factor in the other $47 million that was being taken out of the market each year. In fact the losses figure has diminished even further over time. Yet it took nearly two years to get approval from the company to buy into the concept of this new approach to security. Once implemented and achieved, it had a profound effect on the culture of the operating company, and the confidence of shareholders. It added value to the company's goodwill and reputation, well beyond the local borders.

On a smaller scale but nevertheless a significant piece of value learning, a company headquarters began a business continuity evaluation of critical processes, and realised that certain documents – policies, tax records, contracts, were too valuable to risk storing in an archive without copying them in case of total loss. They began a process to store copies elsewhere. However, once minds were engaged, the question was raised – why, if other documents were not considered valuable, were they being stored at all? A destruction program for the less-important documents resulted in the freeing up of valuable high-cost office space and storage space which could be diverted to higher value activities. Small scale steps like this can build up to large scale results.

After the 2003 invasion of Iraq, a global corporation's top priority was the security of its employees and their families. It immediately triggered its crisis management team covering 13 countries in the Middle East out of Dubai. The team worked on the ground and utilised international intelligence and advice, often pre-empting their input. Its operation was so successful that other multinational organisations sought its advice as well. It moved people quickly to safe havens, making sure employees and their families were not separated. It closed offices where necessary, yet maintained excellent cooperation with suppliers and distributors throughout the region. This ensured that the business kept functioning safely and sensibly with no significant loss of business or distribution.

In the corporation's annual general meeting, the Chairman said that security added value to the business by being an integral part of it, rather than working on its fringes. It was central to building alliances and enabling the sharing of values.

For a long time, anyone from a specialist security function or background offering to discuss the role of security as a business or value multiplier would have been regarded as speaking outside their area of competence and experience. But in the very best companies today, it is increasingly being recognised that investment in security provides additional foundations to produce and deliver better products and services, profitably. Security is no longer the domain only of former public sector security professionals. It is becoming a part of the portfolio and arsenal of other qualified organisation and functional leaders. Outset security provides further benefits to those prepared to invest time and money in testing its viability.

Management guru Peter Drucker once said in the *Harvard Business Review*, "The most important area for developing new concepts, methods, and practices, will be in the management of society's knowledge resources".

What you know in the context of where you operate has great value, which sounds obvious, yet put another way, it can point to significant gaps in asset management. Early in Carla

Fiorina's watch at Hewlett Packard, an internal research programmme revealed that in some ways the company no longer knew what it once knew, and vast amounts of knowledge were hidden in the infrastructure. This was both impractical and costly. The out-take was to realise that the development of "rigorous methods for getting and analysing information is a major challenge for business and information experts."

On an ideological level, you could argue that organisations that have forgotten their past cannot have a future. In the internet age, obsolescence may be seen as a major obstacle to growth. Again it's about how we see things. How one acts as the intelligence strategist in an organisation is critical to its future – getting people to understand this is a different matter, especially if they are in a hurry.

Let's begin with another challenging question – where is the knowledge the security leader needs?

There is a strategic need to capture actionable data and translate it into knowledge which will have both a commercial value and which will enhance corporate reputation. This is the business end of viewing the Secure Value Diagram.

"Secure Value Curve"

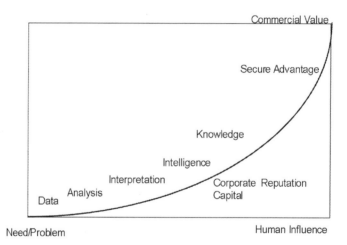

The challenge is in getting the data in the first place, and in making its capture exciting and enjoyable. Just because an idea is being transmitted around the business has no bearing on its adoption, or socialisation. The very idea of a socialisation system, or network, is critical to the idea of stimulating security knowledge and creating learning.

In the early days of smartphones, a US photocopier company gave its field force high-end mobiles so they could get data to the centre for processing more easily, and control call management. What they didn't spot for a while was that experienced engineers started to call each other directly on a job where they didn't know what to do, and they started sharing knowledge through their mobiles. They even began to socialise more, as they found it useful to meet and swap experiences and know-how, becoming better at the job and getting happier customers. The parent company eventually benefited, but it didn't start out with this in mind.

As the extent of human interaction with security matters increases, and this becomes socialised, the ability to capture and manage the benefits should improve, so intangible value can be accumulated and turned into sustainable commercial value. What begins as a controlling function can become a customer relationship builder and a profit deliverer.

This is an illustration of the criticality of moving from the uncertainties of unvalued or unrealised data to the value of a Secure Advantage. We will visit this idea again later. Ultimately, it will be the organisation's ability to align formal security management systems and the socialisation systems in and across an operating culture that will realise the creation of fresh corporate capital and commercial value.

Those who know this already are well on the way to being in the golden circle of Secure Advantage Practitioners. For those bringing new or different skills to senior security roles, there is a significant opportunity for security and security leaders to benefit from these other experiences.

In pioneering enterprises and societies, we note that security is slowly but surely becoming a more professionalised and 'certificated', or chartered, area of business, not simply one where former military or law enforcement officers bring a few of their repackaged ideas and practices with them in to the business domain. This is a development and practice we totally endorse and support, believing there can be no real losers from pursuing this route.

Of course, there are several other levels of development that can be witnessed around the world, so here we explore this a little further, beginning with the belief that:

Corporate Security is to Companies what National Security is to Nations.[2]

"It is amazing how fast and how effectively you can construct a nationality with a flag, a few speeches, and a national anthem."[3]

But what makes a nation state?[4]

Both nation states and multinationals share needs and compete simultaneously. Greater opportunities bring greater risks, as the spectacular collapse of 'Icarus-like' business models testifies, or risk-taking at the state level backfires. To avoid clashes between open-source giants and entrenched corporate and state organisations, there is a need to understand more about the benefits that can be developed from co-operation. To do this requires an acceptance that security has an important role to play in supporting further empowerment, and that this must be a shared resource.

For nation states, a short spread of signifiers might also include the following – its land, currency, governance, ambassadors, community, and shared values.

When you turn to a multinational company, the signifiers look similar – country of origin, brand identity, languages, currency, governance, board, community, and shared values. Some very large companies were also created with great speed.

Such attempts to define *identity* may be highly esoteric to quantitative analysts, but they do form the basis of narratives which appear to motivate people to action, even if the underlying truths about people generally and individuals in particular may be very different. Again, we are motivated to construct stories, and respond to them. Trends and stories affect the behaviour and 'emotions' of global companies too, so while there are Japanese, American, European or other global companies, they are actually based on compromised foundations i.e., they are nationally biased, and although they live in equal markets, some markets are more equal than others.[5]

Identities affect our judgement.

Let's look some of the challenges in these narrative contexts.

Nation states are under pressure. This comes from at least these kinds of areas – stateless global corporations, multinational institutions, the internet and the 'end' of geography, privatisation, town versus country, the decentralisation of values, and sometimes the 'Americanisation' of values.

We are also witnessing the growth of 'We-Think', driven by social networking sites like 'Linkedin', 'Facebook', and 'YouTube', where individuals are developing new ways to innovate and be creative en masse, where you can be organised without an intrusive organisation, and where people can combine skills and ideas without a traditional hierarchy[6]. There are whole new virtual worlds – like Second Life, Habbo Hotel, Entropia Universe, or World of Warcraft waiting for you to enter.

Some kinds of multinational companies are also coming under pressure from emerging states' ambitions, changes in local compliance, a resurgence of local values, the reduction of low cost options, state interference, and brand and target segmentation, within a range of other challenges.

Sir Isaac Newton would state a law of global marketing as "To every global action, there is an equal and opposite reaction, in time". Look at the localisation of Coca-Cola, or foreign inward investment and the Irish character through the years of the Celtic Tiger.

The original point of the industrial economy was mass production for mass consumption, a technique understood and developed by states and religions alike. In the emerging model the point is less about consumption than about voluntary participation. Co-operative and collaborative values are on the march. This is a quiet rebellion against those who believe that to be organised needs a controlling organisation. Some go further, defining an emerging form of 'market state', where the onus to grow and be competitive is down to individuals, the state merely providing the means for individuals to maximise their own potential.[7] It is very much the opposite of the idea of universal welfare based on nannying.

Against this undercurrent, both developed and emerging nation states and multinationals share needs and compete simultaneously. There is a need to understand more about the benefits that can be developed from co-invention and the recognition that consumers already have a higher degree of enabling skills or empowerment in developed countries than ever before. To do this requires an acceptance that security has an important role to play in supporting further empowerment, and that this must be a shared resource.

"The enemy of security is complexity."[8]

For both the state and the corporation, there is a need to be clear in a world of clutter, where decolonisation, new alliances, mergers and break-ups require a full-time monitoring service just to keep up with pace of change.

The increase in the potential mobility of people as well as capital means that the 'war for talent' and the demand for resources will also need new skills and competences. In an accelerating rate-of-change world, there will be a greater need to get people to catch up with who you are and what you stand for, since past stereotypes can create a dangerous lag effect on attitudes and attention.

There is increasingly a need to be iconic and understand that an enabled consumer or participant in your offer is going to be seeking a bargain from their own perspective as equals. On top of this will remain the need to be able to respond to problems and negative publicity with new levels of transparency, efficiency, and honesty, still difficult demands for many giant-sized players.

The events of October 2008 reveal the nature of the challenge very well. "Financial institutions are based on trust, which can only flourish if governments ensure that they are transparent and constrained in the risks they take with other people's money."[9]

All these supports for the state or corporate organism need both internal and external marketing and communication programmes. More than that, they need to be created and nurtured in a secure environment that can deliver added value. Again, this is a world where concepts of brands, and values like trust, play more important roles, and where people are well equipped to understand and respond to the messages and relationships being cultivated by the 'brand' owners. Public servants are often troubled by commercial language and reject marketing terms, yet simultaneously find themselves increasingly in positions where they need to embrace the experience of successful commercial operators to justify the investment required for their objectives and goals to their new managements. The international public servant with an MBA is an emerging model or type.

Some of the challenges for nation states and companies in this noisy world include being able to develop a clear position versus other contenders for their potential customers' attention. This is sometimes easier in smaller environments, like the City of London, or Singapore, or for niche companies, like Connolly Leather, or Porsche. Being known for something truly focused or special also helps, like Switzerland, or Finland, Absolut or Chanel. Having an 'attractor' value is critical to turn lookers into users, among tourists, export purchasers, investors, workers, students, retirees, and other potential customer organisations.

Interest in shoppers visiting Moroccan souks has changed significantly and favourably since the King introduced new thinking about the ways in which shop owners and their colleagues can solicit passers-by to come and look at their goods. In the old days you could guarantee being plagued by people wanting to introduce you to their many 'cousins' who had great products and deals for you in their stalls. It was particularly distressing for some Western women (by and large), who resented this kind of approach, found it intimidating, and relentless. The new hands-off approach, sadly enforced through threats of imprisonment for detractors, is actually proving to be a significant breakthrough in attracting potential high-spenders to the markets. It's a win-win-scenario for those who comply.

Multinationals too must continue to develop clear positions in respect of geography and countries they operate in. This means building an even greater understanding of what it means to be known for something, good and bad, and attracting the same kinds of targets as the nation states. This goes beyond managing a set of brands and products and includes managing the corporate brand more as well.

National images and impressions are formed through their history, people, culture, ceremony, visual icons, achievements, products and brands, transportation, and traits and values. These are major, but clearly not comprehensive, elements.

A secure environment plays a critical role in the image creation. Once again, it is very similar for multinationals. Their history, products and brands, visual icons, strategic alliances, corporate social responsibility, and their approach to security, all contribute to overall image. Hard and soft capabilities, goods and services produced, style of operation, etc., bring different levels of internal and external confidence, which ultimately drive economic performance.

Security is a bed rock for these drivers, and new brands or corporations emerging from developing markets need and do demonstrate to potential customers the same levels of trust they have come to expect in other places.

Security as a foundation in a national marketing or economic growth plan played a key part in helping update Spain's reputation after Franco, the kind of security that leads to freedom not oppression. It helped in repackaging the reputation of South Africa after apartheid.

Marketing with new levels of security drove an updated reputation for Apple, helped create a reputation for Blackberry, and helped repackage a reputation for Skoda. Security is a driving force in the success of leading emerging market manufacturers and service providers.

For most powerful, inclusive visions, we believe security has an added value role to play, because external and internal marketing without secure foundations is like music without instruments. But you could argue that where a multinational corporation can choose its employees a government can't choose its citizens. This can work for you or against you, and even that depends on which perspective you have. A research tool developed by a communications agency to help evaluate brand assets[10] applied a variation to countries in terms of how its own people viewed themselves as a country, a nation, versus others, on two key dimensions – of perceived brand stature, and of brand viability. In other words, how you feel about your status in the world, and how dynamic you regard yourself versus others, are competitive differentiators.

The findings of such research are always interesting, in some cases lending quantitative weight to the subjective observations of people like Thomas Jefferson, who remarked, "Every man has two countries: his own and France".

While nation states and multinational corporations might look different, many agendas now have recognisable common elements, even if agenda management and execution take on very different forms today. It may be time to move to more networked coalitions.

Corporate security and national security should become networked security.

This can be examined further when we look at boundary reduction and productive convergence in public and private sectors.

Whatever the changing status of public and private sectors, we believe in the need to work harder both to recognise and support the productive convergence of security skills and practices across and between these sectors.

It is possible to enhance resource capability, depending on how you engage with Public Private Partnerships, but whatever perspective you have, increased liaison and networking can only be fruitful if the answer to these two questions embraces the acknowledgement that together is better than alone:

- What do we need to know?
- How do we get it?

Even if the answer to the first question is driven by reaction to a shocking and disruptive event, and results in the frustrated statement that "We don't even know what we need to know", the starting point for plans from which improved action can be taken will be stronger if the knowledge base is wider.

Deciding what needs to be known and who needs to know it are two more of the most challenging questions of the day:

- Where do you get 'the known' from?
- How do you get 'the known' known by chosen others?

The Boston Consulting Organisation might have posited this grid for our contemplation:

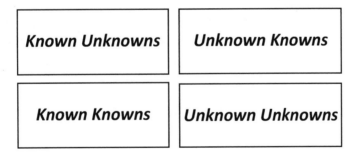

This may make those with strong antipathies to business jargon wince, but there is a value in looking at these questions from a security perspective.

Alternative expressions could be found for those who prefer to work with a more colourful palette, but the principles remain. When these have been collected and collated, the process of getting to meaningful value and sustainable intellectual capital can be undertaken, and can be restated with the Securing Value curve we introduced earlier. This leads us forward to the notion of the Secure Advantage.

"Secure Advantage"

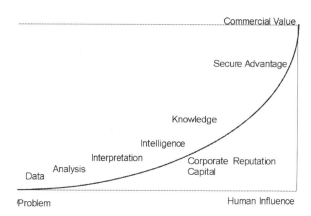

This looks easy to capture as a chart, but appears to exclude the barriers to progress that many people who have tried to achieve this in reality actually encounter.

Let's look at some of these barriers, or blockages, and see how they have affected or delayed outcomes.

Let's begin by observing that of course nothing much seems to have changed at other points in time, so can we really do anything other than throw our arms up in the air?

The Dunkirk evacuation in 1942 was not helped by what might diplomatically be called Anglo-French 'co-operation'. The Dunkirk rear guards' task was made immensely harder by figures like the French general who, when asked to counterattack in support of the only significant British tank offensive at Arras said, "I can do nothing about the (German) tanks". In-fighting between the British and French staffs continued through the evacuation itself.[11]

Commenting on Pearl Harbour, one found it "much easier after the event to sort the relevant from the irrelevant signals. After the event, of course, a signal is always crystal clear; we can now see what disaster it was signalling since the disaster has occurred. But before the event it is obscure and pregnant with conflicting meanings."[12]

The actual 9/11 attacks, according to the 9/11 Commission, revealed four kinds of failures, in:

- imagination
- policy
- capabilities
- management.

They decided it would be "crucial to find a way of routineising, even bureaucratising, the exercise of imagination".

Those analysing Pearl Harbour had gone on to develop methods for detecting and then warning of surprise attacks on the US in the decades following that event. The proposed methods didn't fail – they were not tried by the time it came to analysing who the 9/11 attackers might be. It appears to be a hard task to respect lessons from the past that might have valuable insights for handling threats in the future.

In terms of policy, it is a fact of life that mounting a major effort against what at the time seems like a minor problem is a real barrier. It is the same in industry, with competition. When a danger or threat has fully materialised, evident to all, action becomes easier, but it may be too late. Crisis management should not become the default style of operation, but it does have plus points.

It gets even worse with capabilities, where those responsible for matching capabilities to missions define the tough part of their task away. "They are often passive, accepting what are viewed as givens, including that efforts to identify and fix glaring vulnerabilities to dangerous threats would be too costly, too controversial, or too disruptive".[13]

In *Bush on War*[14] it was noted, "There is a tendency in our planning to confuse the unfamiliar with the improbable... the danger is in a poverty of expectations, a routine obsession with a few dangers that may be familiar rather than likely."

The best and most revealing piece of the Commission's report is in their appraisal of Operational Management:

"Information was not shared, sometimes inadvertently or because of legal misunderstandings. Analysis was not pooled. Effective operations were not launched. Often the handoffs of information were lost across the divide separating the foreign and domestic agencies of the government ... the agencies are like a set of specialists in a hospital, each ordering tests, looking for symptoms, and prescribing medications. What is missing is the attendant physician who makes sure they work as a team."

Yes, there are organisational challenges relating to information collection and collation, dissemination and action planning, execution and archiving, but there is only one longstanding and overriding truth – there are no business problems, there are only people problems.

So back to one of the world's most powerful men: George W Bush would have loved to have seen a world defined by Thomas Gradgrind in the appropriately named *Hard Times*:[15]

"Now, what I want is Facts....Facts alone are wanted in life."

You are either in charge or you are not, you are in control or you are not. "You are either with us, or you are against us". Sadly this does not reflect that we all live in a world where life, and the language we use to describe it, is full of more subtle conditionals.

Security takes on the task of trying to make sense of the conditional.

A world-class security leader and team should be able to lend clarity to scenarios like those described, within any organisation. One of the ways of tackling this kind of challenge is to use services that provide a quantitative and qualitative information source to help management get a bigger and better view on how to deal with conditional circumstances across many markets.

It takes special, taught skills plus experience, to deal with the unknown and random with intellectual honesty. It is un-natural, or seems to be, to go through life making totally confident claims about the future, when you look at the evidence, but then most people don't get that close, so promises of a golden future become the norm, and people follow those that promise it, from religious leaders to hedge fund managers.

It is not possible to capture all the sources of uncertainty. The smart operator deals with the possibilities of things, not simply with the timing of the probability of things. Yet the world has a number of folks who made a fortune from only working with probabilities – that's another way of handling risk. Normal i.e. untrained folks, overestimate what is known, and underestimate uncertainty, by compressing the range of uncertain states. We are naturally wired up to try to reduce the space of the unknown, or align with people who promise they can do that for us or with us.

It gets worse. Once we have a theory about the way things are, we find it very difficult to change our minds, so one of the principles of this book, the need to embrace change, turns out to be an un-natural request. It actually feels uncomfortable. The same holds for opinions, which we appear to form very quickly, and revise significantly more slowly, even if new information comes along that is clearly more accurate. "We treat ideas like possessions, and it will be hard for us to part with them."[16]

Admiral Bill Owens also noted, "Once devised in Riyadh (in 1991), the tasking order took six hours to get to the Navy's six aircraft carriers – because the Navy had failed years earlier to procure the proper communications gear that would have connected the Navy with its Air Force counterparts...To compensate for the lack of communications capability, the Navy was forced to fly a daily cargo mission from the Persian Gulf and Red Sea to Riyadh in order to pick up a computer printout of the air mission tasking order, then fly back to the carriers, run photocopy machines at full speed, and then distribute the document to the air wing squadrons that were planning the next strike."[17]

This is not an outstanding example of the benefits of convergence.

The *Oxford English Dictionary* offers this definition of convergence – "coming together from different directions to meet". It implies doing this sensibly, although of course it includes the interpretation of crashing. We would like to stay on the more positive end of the scale, utilising such positive interpretations as co-operation, integration, synergy, togetherness, and team work.

Convergence, or the constant consideration of it, should not be regarded merely in the context of security but as a fundamental driver of organisational productivity. The benefits of convergence should be analysed in any situation where understanding, co-operation and inter-dependability is crucial.

Of course, it comes in many different forms. There is the 'conscious competence' form of convergence, like that that eventually made international banking exchange systems viable, motor manufacturing assembly systems practical, international package delivery manageable, and universal coordinated time (UCT) possible.

There are forms of 'unconscious competence' in convergence which have pervaded the world of technology – "The innovations (of the information revolution) have occurred largely without central direction or a clear game plan, and the effects of the revolution in the way we communicate will continue... we are only beginning to see purposeful efforts to channel the power in these technologies in support of good governance or effective and expedient management."

Then of course there is 'conscious incompetence', the absence of positive convergence, which can be seen many times where there is a major security scare in the air transport business, where chaos and confusion enter as joint chiefs in a world of disconnected contingency plans, and a lack of cooperation between governments, public and private operators, airlines and airport authorities. In these circumstances, there are missed opportunities, a loss of value, brand erosion, and considerably weakened customer confidence and respect. A lack of convergence and integration even exposes operators to ridicule.

In this emerging picture:

- Does the security function have a role to play in bringing values to relevant levels of convergence?

- Do you see business integrated security, and specifically IT security within that sphere, as a help or hindrance to successful dispersed operators and operations?

If we take further the notion that corporate security is to companies what national security is to nations, what will drive more convergence?

The growth in computer-based crime required a broader security understanding and investigative skills. This has driven the need for acceptable and admissible computer-based evidence in what were traditional security investigations. Emerging and developing investigative skills need to continue to cross-pollinate, which also facilitates better public sector law enforcement collaboration and engagement.

Corporate governance is enhanced through convergence because IT security is separated from being a subordinate position in the overall delivery of IT into a role which focuses on identifying and eliminating conflicts of interest. This simultaneously promotes the validation and support of unpopular but necessary IT controls. In most cases, convergence elevates IT security to being a direct report to a head of function, which in turn provides better career prospects and motivations for IT security managers.

At the macro level, convergent IT and communication technologies can benefit culture, science, and the quality of life in general. Yet with every benefit there is a flip-side – at the same time they can also serve up aggression, violence, pornography, crime, and extremism. Lastly, and in line with that other trend, they can empower individuals over nation states, and small organisations over large, where the creation of identity is being individualised.

This challenges the 'community of sentiment' that used to be a key constituent of nation state and corporate cultures. Nation states and corporations have been standardisers of laws, language and beliefs, the constructors of historical memories that provide foundational myths for their continuing existence. New balances are required to keep these territorial and trading worlds in line with both the freedoms and the threats that a growing band of empowered individuals constitutes. In pursuit of balance, it is critical to emphasise that convergence does *not* equal centralisation and demands for more centralised controls.

Power shifts in enlightened communities should create a greater balance between central and hierarchical structure on the one hand, and individuals and dispersed organisations on the other hand. It is clear that criminally minded types have in many cases grasped the implications of this faster than legitimate enterprises and their 'centrist' backlash rushes to claim the need for more power and control. The way forward is not through more rules and inhibitions delivered centrally.

Central command and control experts' error rates in judging the likelihood of a range of events in general political, economic, and military areas within a specified timeframe of about five years ahead are very often well ahead of their own estimations. On the occasions when they are right, they attribute it to their own depth of understanding and expertise. When wrong it is either the situation or circumstances that are to blame, or, worse still, they refuse to recognise they are wrong and try to spin out of it. This is called self-protection. So we attribute successes to our skills, and failures to external events beyond our control, often to randomness. This means many people think they are better than others at what they do for a living. This is endemic in many public service environments.

In an amusing, anonymous and insightful book,[18] a Mr David Copperfield deduces that in the UK police there are no bad ideas, only good ideas that fail because of 'a lack of resource', e.g. "It is impossible to implement effective policing because of a lack of funding", which he interprets as meaning "Leave me alone, I only want to collect my pension as soon as possible."

'He' notes that millions of pounds and thousands of man hours go on coming up with innumerable policy documents, plans to cover every eventuality, and a so-called audit trail, so that every last detail of force performance can be monitored by central government. The effect is to ensure that new ideas are implemented on the basis of how well they comply with regulations, rather than how well they deal with criminals and prevent crime.

Elsewhere he sarcastically records that there seems to be a belief in the senior ranks that technology will be able to make up for bad management. "If the police had designed email, each would cost £1 and take a week to be delivered. Meanwhile, a printout of the contents of the email would have to be sent via the ordinary post to a depot in the force area where the email was sent from. Then it would be filed with accompanying forms".

He sums it up well by saying that the problem is in how the force is deployed and used, not in the lack of resource numbers or funding. The same applies for the perennial demand for more powers. Robert Peel appeared to get the balance in his enlightened *Nine principles of policing*, which includes this:

"Seven. The police, at all times, should maintain a relationship with the public that gives reality to the historic tradition that the police are the public and the public are the police; the police being only members of the public who are paid to give full-time attention to duties which are incumbent on every citizen in the interests of community welfare and existence".

An expert will no doubt pronounce this form of Victorian idealism is of no relevance to today's dysfunctional and specialised society, whose citizens "have a firm belief in the primacy of their own rights at the expense of everyone else's".

Governments and large corporations can both suffer from this form of 'expertise' and perspective management. For many it is more profitable to pull the whole organisation together and go in the wrong direction than to be alone in the right direction.

"New forms of digital diplomacy, networked and technology driven, will need to be developed and mastered by organisations able to manage challenges with speed, flexibility, reach and efficiency." [19] The only thing to add to this is the need to respect the contribution of the individual to navigating a secure future.

Convergence of this nature will make more demands on human skills like motivation and leadership,

Ultimately, and in keeping with a key theme of this book:

More convergence enhances trust through transparency, which is, or should be, a core business and organisational value.

Invest in preparedness, not in prediction.[20]

Security is a significant area of unrealised incremental value today.

The mission is to make security management a competitive asset.

Corporate Security is to Companies what National Security is to Nations.

Corporate security and national security should become networked security.

Security takes on the task of trying to make sense of the conditional.

More convergence enhances trust through transparency, which is, or should be, a core business and organisational value.

Security is not an option. It is a right.

---

5. Security and Shareholder Value

What critical factors will affect companies trying to be competitive over the next decade? What is the feasibility and relevance of security in addressing these challenges? In answering these questions, we re-enter the world of intangible as well as tangible value.

"As manufacturing technology moves more and more freely across borders, it will become harder and harder for any company to gain a competitive edge or advantage just by making things".[1] Comparative advantage will come from areas like design and marketing, branding and distribution, and micro marketing opportunities.

Gaining and keeping an edge will come from companies that can excel at producing things that are difficult to copy. In a world where copying and counterfeiting is getting quicker and more sophisticated, differences may come through things other than the goods produced themselves. They may be in services, or styles of service, individualised. Value becomes less about execution alone, and more about conception and perception. It's about relative experiences. Brands that succeed will be able to generate fresh ideas that make you feel better through your relationship with them and vice versa in a tacit way. But not every brand has a future simply by declaring, "Use me and you'll feel good". The challenge then is to identify and assess the potential of motivating ideas, which are often intangible, and translate these into sustainable value.

Those who manage to do this then face the next challenge, which is how to protect all this, strategically. This is probably not something the John Wayne or Clint Eastwood type of Protector in the movies would have warmed to.

Branded goods, and especially those that command a premium, have the ability to let consumers believe they are getting better value and authenticity. Even the buyers of superior fakes believe this, as they imbue the products with brand values. Legitimate choice and freedom to choose extend this model.[2] Brand values become more tied up with values about service.

What distinguishes service? This is about the quality and combination of image and experience you have through your chosen brand. It is decided by the kind of relationship you have with it, over time, through place(s), and the pleasure and rewards you get and feel. So, for example, a great hotel may well be distinguished by virtue of its stunning location, but you will credit it as much for the quality of service you received, often from one particular and memorable person, which gives the total experience an added value.

When products are at parity, distribution is similar, and pricing is equal, the remaining competitive weapon for the brand owner is the quality of the relationship it has with its customers.

In the old days, engineers would proudly pronounce that their products were simply the best in the business. "We are engineering minded... not fanatical about the business side". The CEO of the same company, Embraer Aircraft, now says this. "When you've only got 100 customers, you have to focus entirely on *what they want*". By the way, Embraer is the fourth largest airplane maker in the world, and the market expects to sell nearly 10,000 business jets costing some $144 billion over the next decade.[3]

A long time ago BMW cars were excellent, if you could afford the options, but you needed a strong will to get anything like a reasonable level of service from showroom staff, people who appeared to believe that the cars bestowed on them a justifiable level of superiority over mere customers. Reputation suffered for some time. Especially if you happened to be a woman. Women with cash visiting showrooms with boyfriends, husbands or simply male friends and colleagues were systematically ignored by sales*men* who immediately addressed themselves to the present male.

Having waited over an hour for a main course to follow a completed starter, the maitre d' telling you and your esteemed guests that "The chef is a busy man, you know" has not credited the perceived service value greatly.

The airline saying there are no delays to your flight, knowing the said aircraft is still on the ground at the departure point of the destination you are trying to get to is not scoring significantly on the goodwill it might need for a really bad moment (although many airlines now seem to be immune to the need to give passengers a 'quality experience' of any kind). The Dutch Airline that answers the phone by giving its name and then says "Cargo and Passengers, how may we help?" at least unwittingly alerts you to its priorities.

Brands need to manage the whole length of the shadows they cast. The kinds of relationships strong brands need to nurture must be strategically secure. The conditions under which the relationships are conducted become as critical as the contents. Ideas and images also travel through services, and these media require management and protection as well. There is a powerful role for security here as a critical success factor in the durability of brands and their controlling organisations.

Successful security management comes through balancing organisation responsibility and individual freedom, and needs to respect this position, as a pervasive and positive force for its customers and consumers. One example would be creating a security-derived strategy for hotels which help women understand they get security designed specifically for their needs. This can then help to maintain the attraction of high-spenders to the sites.

Within the brand owning organisation itself, security needs to be flexible enough to demonstrate an equal competence in corporate governance.

Recent studies[4] we have seen show that companies with recognised corporate governance command a significant share premium. The practices and processes of governance make good business sense and can be value-adding in themselves.

Security has a key role to perform in the critical activities of the Board that involve issues of governance like:

- Risk management
- Assurance control
- Supply and flow of information.

How these are managed affects shareholders, colleagues, and communities alike. Hewlett-Packard's experiences in this area, with the battle between Patricia Dunn and Tom Perkins, were a text book case of how not to handle governance professionally. That company had a series of setbacks and then settled down, changing its style and practice and additionally taking comfort from the fact that research also indicated investments in companies with the highest quality of governance structures and behaviour significantly outperform those with the lowest. This goes hand-in-hand with the fact that the higher the corporate governance score, the lower the equity-price volatility.

Companies with the top 20% of governance scores are more profitable than those within the bottom 20%. Finally, while the bottom 20% show an average return on equity (ROE) of 1.5%, the top 20% show an average ROE of 15.9% in the same year.

Risk management is about taking risks responsibly, and clearly involves risk identification, risk assessment and analysis, and risk mitigation. This is a complex area, which needs to be comprehensive, and needs be related to "market, credit, liquidity, technological, legal, health, safety, environment, reputation and business priority issues" (according to *Turnbull Guidance*, from the UK).

The poor management of risk has a negative impact on the achievement of business objectives and ultimately on shareholder value.

The consequences of poor risk management can be seen through:

- Direct Losses: project failures, litigation costs, irrecoverable asset or fund transfer, unexpected staff costs, regulatory penalties, physical damage and theft, interruptions in the supply chain, breaks in business continuity
- Indirect Losses: brand value erosion or reputation damage, loss of market share, loss of key staff, loss of key customers, increased insurance costs
- Opportunity costs: lost opportunities to enter new markets or develop new products, to leverage the latest technologies, to gain a competitive edge.

Security's role in this array of good governance requirements should be:

- To be a seamless and efficient brand and equity value contributor to the risk management function and team, not merely a subordinate process
- Owned by everyone in risk management's operating circle
- With Quantitative and Qualitative contributions
- Definably a set of behaviours and attitudes.

The bottom line here is that security should not be bought in or overlaid on existing corporate functional processes. As the *Turnbull Guidance* says of governance, we say of security strategy and execution:

Security must be embedded in the operations of the company and form part of its culture.

Security is part of an organisation's DNA.

Employee communication and education is a strategic necessity. Each individual needs to be empowered to identify, assess, and treat security issues that are within their sphere of control. In the old days, brand owners wanted consumers to worship at the altar of the brands they created. These days security, like a brand, needs to justify its place in the context of people's lives, to which it may give added meaning or value, but as a means, not as a defining object.

Brands rarely come with complex rulebooks – ok, forget the printer... and equally, security should not be achieved through the application of complex rules and defensive sign-offs. Common sense and trust are the most important factors in building secure value, which, like a brand itself, is developed in the same way, through communications and relationships.

Management needs to ensure the holistic treatment of security issues.

Physical, personnel, and electronic security are all linked today, and in this world, rather than attempting to teach people the right things to do, the organisation should be designed such that doing the right things is the path of least resistance to growth, admirable performance, and enviable reputation.

We repeat – security and shareholder value are inextricably linked in the most successful companies. What can be done to apply this learning in your own organisation, or the one you have invested in, or influence, or all three?

Security has a significant role to play in debates along the lines of – Who audits the auditors? There are long running debates about auditing practice and objectivity today, and it seems, for always. Here are some examples of the make-up of the debates:

- The ethos of British auditing is that the approach encourages auditors to think about what they are doing and use their judgement. In the USA, if a crook is smart enough to appear to follow the rules, the auditor will tick the boxes.[5]

- But if legislation reforms come into effect, what auditor is going to risk his judgement in marginal cases if he thinks criminal law could be used against him if he turns out to be wrong? This will lead to safety play for strong clients and a refusal to work for clients that appear to be financially troubled. The number of truly objective audit reports will fall as the profession covers itself. The net result will be fewer businesses and more unnecessary failures, not better auditing or investor protection.

Internationally, The Big Four accounting firms appear to often almost 'monopolise' the auditing of a whole gamut of companies, bolstered by the trust investors and bankers who keep willingly placing faith in their alleged rigour, experience and reach. The perception is that The Big Four's work is a cut above that of other domestic accounting firms.

Domestic or international, obviously audit firms are charged with playing a key role in mitigating the risks of investing in companies and countries. In the capital markets particularly, the prevailing view is that The Big Four are streets ahead in terms of professionalism, technical ability, and their independence from clients. But as in most developed markets, they have all been embroiled in their share of controversies. Not only that, potential conflicts of interest appear when the same firms' consulting divisions are significantly involved with the same businesses.

The biggest gap in the auditing world is not about international versus local levels of competence, it is about objectivity, and The Big Four's promise of a consistent global service linked to their ability to deliver it on the ground.[6]

Independence is compounded by the nature of the client paying the auditor directly. Perhaps independence is not the key issue. The core issue is probably more about the integrity of the auditors and the transparency and completeness of their findings and conclusions.

The French government is insisting that auditing companies cannot simultaneously provide consulting services to the same clients. This is a trend that should and will probably grow. We believe that the core principles and practices of the kind of added value corporate security we are advocating should also be applied to building better levels of transparency between auditors and their clients, so that both auditors and shareholders are less subject to surprises, disasters, losses, and punitive comebacks.

The poor management of risk has a negative impact on the achievement of business objectives and ultimately on shareholder value.

Security must be embedded in the operations of the company and form part of its culture.

Security is part of an organisation's DNA.

---

6. Getting Even More from Your Investment in Security

Working globally, with many of the world's largest and most respected companies, we are sharing proven experiences and practices that can help an organisation realise incremental benefits and value from a shift in the way investment in security is regarded.

In today's environment, while security in a small number of world-class companies is becoming a core activity, it is still regarded by many simply as a cost of doing business, a transaction cost. We need to be committed to changing this perception with tangible results.

Here are some examples of how significantly reduced insurance premiums can be obtained, and how other areas of value for the organisation can be enhanced.

One multinational organisation managed kidnap and ransom as a multifunctional activity led by corporate security. Instead of effectively abrogating all responsibility to kidnap and ransom consultants, it adopted a policy that the company itself had to be not only aware, but fully trained on a continuous basis to deal with any kidnap scenario arising. From the centre and in each region, multifunctional crisis management teams were regularly briefed on global practices and patterns among criminal organisations. They undertook scenario-based management exercises in organisations that also included representatives of law enforcement and security services, crisis psychologists and insurance representatives. Apart from the advantage that the company was better prepared to handle and manage actual incidents, it was also able to secure the input of specialist consultancies more effectively. Because of the significantly reduced risk from an insurance perspective it was able to secure insurance premiums some 40% less than other equivalent companies with no diminution in service levels at all. Victims, hostages, and families also received a more professionally managed service within the familiarity of the corporation and its culture.

Exactly the same benefits accrued when the practice was extended to malicious product contamination scenarios, and the chances of harm to the public and the company from both the perspective of reputation and continuing value were further reduced.

Integrated business security can not only prevent the loss of substantial revenues, but it can facilitate essential business roles in risk management for major multinational clients through to locally focused businesses.

Answers to the following kinds of questions can enhance the role, quality and contribution of security in a business. If you are a senior management figure, ask yourself:

- Do you rate security within your own organisation in the same way you rate other business roles and functions?

- How can you know you are taking advantage of best practices in security throughout your business?

- How can you get better value out of the relationships between specialists like audit, IT, risk, compliance, marketing and sales and other necessary roles for which security plays a paramount role?

- How can you audit the fitness, efficiency and contribution of security itself to the overall goals and values of the business?

Security no longer lives in isolation. For the best security professionals it never has, and it remains a lifelong challenge to master, to integrate new learning, and to help others understand the real potential for security in the organisation. This is made more of a challenge by the often intangible elements of good security practice.

Security can be hard to tie down. It is not simply a thing, or a system, or just a department, yet it embraces those elements. It overlaps with many functions that feel they own the better or more profitable elements of the security contribution. It can be a turf war soldier, and sometimes a victim. It is more like an organism, living in a collective, not in isolation. As Bruce Schneier observes[1] security is "...just one component of a complicated transaction. It costs money but it can also cost in intangibles; time, convenience, flexibility, and privacy." These are just as much human dimensions as functions of factory based efficiency and need. Security is an element in the make-up of what constitutes an operation's assets.

In the established, protective security world, Schneier provides a practical process to analyse and evaluate security, which he expands on out of five key steps:

1. What assets are you trying to protect?
2. What are the risks to those assets?
3. How well does the security solution mitigate those risks?
4. What other risks does the security solution cause?
5. What costs and trade-offs does the security solution impose?

He goes on to posit an additional question "Is the security solution worth it?" This is sound practice, and security practitioners who end up with satisfactory answers and solutions to these will more than likely be doing a professional job. Where we step in is to say that having got to this stage, can any more questions be legitimately asked about security's role and potential?

The answer is yes, and beyond the fact that Schneier himself states that there is no single correct level of security, even in the protective role alone. He goes on, "Different people have different senses of what constitutes a threat, or what level of risk is acceptable... most security decisions are complicated, involving multiple players with their own subjective assessments of security. Moreover, each of these players also has his own agenda, often having nothing to do with security, and some amount of power in relation to other players."

Everyone looks at security from his or her own perspective and position. In moving security's potential incremental contribution further, the contemporary security professional is going to have to work harder to unravel the knots that can occur in an organisation's network between enlightened self-interest and value-enabling security.

Security is always going to be about more than its literal definitions. Managing and nurturing security for the good of the organisation requires a sturdy appreciation of variations of such personal development exercises as 'The Prisoner's Dilemma'. As a final nod in the direction of Mr Schneier, he acknowledges that "security is situational, subjective, and social".

As security systems, at least technology-based ones, become more sophisticated, and in some cases more efficient and effective, attacks on assets must come through exploring opportunities in weaker links in an enterprise's security value-chain. Perhaps unsurprisingly, these are likely to focus more and more on the softest side of the security equation, the human factor.

"The human factor is the weakest link."[2]

Social engineers is a label for those who through the ages have understood, learned, and applied ways to take advantage of fundamentally unchanged aspects of human nature, which people in organisations need to be taught about repeatedly in order to improve their ability to recognise and handle. It is a recurring cultural issue.

Someone who wants information can get it in any number of ways. "It's just a matter of time, persistence, patience, and personality." Who needs to even begin to worry about 1024 levels of encryption when six phone calls will get a company's staff competing to help you get the vital information you need?

Out there are masters of understanding human and technological re-engineering. For instance, they know that corporate security is a question of balance for most enterprises. "Too little security leaves you vulnerable, but an overemphasis on traditional security gets in the way of attending to business, inhibiting the company's growth and prosperity. The challenge is to achieve a balance between security and productivity". And it is in the seams of these that the expert attacker operates. In fact, one expert in this area sums it up beautifully by stating, "Trust is the key to deception". [3]

In a world where the pressure is on getting a job done now, security is often seen as the tortoise in the race to clinch the next sale or deal. In fact, trust is a risk condition, a principle that security more than most other functions should be best positioned to understand and manage.

In this world, people make judgements based on appearance, and in those places where smoke and mirrors play tricks, the social engineer makes his magic. The magnitude of this threat cannot be overestimated. According to *Computer World* magazine, an analysis at a New York-based Fund Management company led to a startling discovery. The firm's Vice President of Network Security and Disaster Recovery ran a password attack against the employees of his firm using one of the standard software packages. The magazine reported that within three minutes he managed to crack the passwords of 800 employees

It's not enough for employees to know the security policies and procedures. They need to understand how important these policies are to the company in terms of damage prevention, survivability and growth.

Companies that conduct security penetration tests report that their attempts to break into client computer systems by social engineering are nearly 100% successful.

Dr Robert Cialdini[4] writing about manipulation of the social engineering kind, summarised research in this area by presenting "six basic tendencies of human nature" that social engineers capitalise on. These are:

1. Authority
2. Liking
3. Reciprocation
4. Consistency
5. Social Validation
6. Scarcity.

The core tenet of any security awareness programme needs to be to influence people to change their behaviour and attitudes. They need to be motivated to want to be involved and do their part to protect the organisation's assets. It needs to show that not wanting to adopt a culture adjusted for security's enhanced role is to miss opportunities for the enterprise and themselves in a mutually reinforced way. This is a true management challenge, since in most organisations there are few subjects that everyone needs to understand that are simultaneously as important and as dull as protective versus James Bond-style security. The best programmes need to inform and engage to capture both the attention and the enthusiasm and commitment of the learners.

One of the major reasons for our advocacy of security as an enabling tool as well as a protective agent is that by making security a more actively demonstrable contributor to organisational value, getting the appropriate amount of attention from every level, it serves both to drive new levels of interest in security's potential for the greater good, and raises the bar for the tolerance and subsequent adoption of basic security practices.

Nine out of every ten large corporations and government agencies have been hit by computer attackers, but only one company in three reports or publicly acknowledges any attacks.[5] Not surprisingly, since most companies prefer not to lose customer confidence or announce their vulnerability to like-minded attackers. Social engineering attacks have not even been surveyed comprehensively, or at least any findings published, to our knowledge. The chances are that even more companies don't even know they've been attacked in this way.

There are comprehensive guides to developing corporate information security policies, and a wealth of case studies to illustrate the human dimensions of social engineering that we all recognise, usually post-event.

One of the challenges for security and its management is the way to make it interesting in a positive light. With great modern security nothing happens that you can easily see. It only gets attention when something goes wrong. This is not a path most managers seek in their own careers. Few seek recognition in failure. Security practices can actually teach us a great deal about what managers really want to know without situations spilling over into crisis mode.

Once the boundaries in the security chain have been given as much strength as possible, and it is at the links where most attackers search out weaknesses, it is time to see how security can enhance the jewels, or assets, that are being held together by the chain itself. All are part of the organisation's overall body, health, and systems. As these systems get more complex through global operations, outsourcing partners, multiple distribution channels etc, there is a very strong danger that they increase their exposure to risk.

Security management needs to be able to work with these escalations of threats without slowing down needlessly the enterprise's business. To manage this properly requires considerable human skills, since security's role is often counter-intuitive to people's thoughts and beliefs, and especially where it is not embedded in the operating culture. This is true of a lot of corporate behaviour, as the following example neatly captures:

"Increasingly, people seem to misinterpret complexity as sophistication, which is baffling – the incomprehensible should cause suspicion rather than admiration."[6] This was brought home in significantly tangible ways with the 2008 global financial crisis. Managements of major financial services organisations claimed they didn't understand how their financial products and services worked at any level of detail. They were 'too complex'. You were expected to invest in these same services. Imagine the pilot of your just boarded airplane saying he liked the jet but didn't understand any of the details behind all the flashing lights in the cockpit.

If a person's mind is potentially one of the most important security countermeasures available, more work needs to be done to persuade people that a technology-based security blanket only offers partial protection. Top-rated managers should understand this well from their own position and perspective. Getting them to look at security predicated on their own experiences and competences may well enhance their ability to see security as essentially complementary to their own current and future function, role, contribution, career success and respect.

The challenge for masters of metrics is to devise a way to estimate the value of this intangible idea of 'feeling safe' to organisational productivity. The mathematics of feelings may be too much of a challenge today, but certainly new work in neurosciences is beginning to reveal useful quantitative data in these kinds of areas that were formerly dismissed as un-measurable, or sublimated under other, easier banners to handle.

Work in these areas may also lead to new insights into how to improve the effectiveness of the golden triangle of:

- identification
- authentication
- authorisation.

Imagine the time when brain scans can quickly reveal what part of your neural circuitry lights up when you are shown a picture of someone you are very close to, and how you can't fake that.

As with organisations, the best security evolves. It is Darwinian. In any system there will be those who pay the price for slow adaptation, and those who win the rewards for relevant evolution. In nature, genes take care of much of the task. In a human organisational world, technology change needs to be supported by the key trait of negotiation. You cannot escape from the fact that security management is primarily a social occupation. That doesn't turn it into a cocktail party. A keen sense of the way numbers and statistics drive behaviour and affect perceptions is also a necessary evolutionary survival skill. Most ordinary people are absolutely not on top of the data available to them about risks and threats, and their views are moulded by the media all the time. A numbers-based approach to security, on top of the social skills, will go a long way to supporting the drive to create a world-class security environment for an organisation. From this base the imaginative skills required to create new solutions for emerging challenges can have freer rein.

In one global manufacturing company, the security department proposed a forum in which they would meet with HR, Legal and Audit to discuss cases which might be better resolved by teamwork rather than a single department acting alone. For example, where an internal fraud had been discovered, often previously the miscreant had been quietly dismissed through HR without any attempt to recover the lost assets. This secrecy also prevented the development of better procedures and learning from the experience. The new approach depended vitally on establishing mutual trust among the participants, but in due course the forum paid significant dividends as properly run investigations using the combined skills of the departments' improved business practices across the company and led to the recovery of assets.

How would you value that contribution?

Can this approach work profitably in other areas of co-operative activity?

Here we can look briefly at mergers and acquisitions activities (M&A). In addition to supporting the process of M&A activity through risk management fundamentals, security has an ongoing role to play in supporting the branding and reputation of merging entities, a form of Intellectual Property protection, and security should be judged by the extent of its presence in such strategic issues, not by its absence or 'presence by afterthought'. This is another example of where business outset security can add incremental value to organisations.

One expert reflecting on this topic[7], notes, "The age old question that people have been trying to answer is 'Do acquisitions create value?' You find on average the typical deal does not create value. It is better to look at what *types* of deal create value."

Synergies are posited as the result of the value put on what two companies can do better together than apart. A major value could come through cost savings.[8] The second major value can come through combining complementary strengths, e.g. a better product from one with a superior distribution system from another, as in Procter and Gamble providing products to WalMart. A third area may emerge from process improvements through adopting the best practices of each part. Others may come out of financial re-engineering or tax advantages.

Failures have often occurred because executives have not correctly read the business they were buying into. Research we have seen shows that eight out ten buyers do not plan properly for how the new company will be integrated after acquisition. "In our surveys of the acquisition skills most associated with success, the biggest thing is the clarity with which a company articulates the concrete steps they are going to take after acquisition".

The adrenalin rush to acquire is not matched by the post-possession feeling of ordinariness. Sweeping up after the big match is a job for those who weren't sitting in the directors' boxes during the game. Security needs to be in a position where it isn't reporting to the management that the great game was fixed, but where the game was going to be a thrilling and worthwhile event in the first place. Security will not be embraced by thrill-seekers if its only role is to induce the feeling of being let down by telling you that your selected sporting hero was being sponsored by Steroids Inc. two years and a lot of lost money after the event.

Another challenge is in generating value for the acquiring company's shareholders. In general it seems hard for firms to benefit their owners by buying other firms[9]. First is to avoid having all the value creation flow to the shareholders of the acquired firm. Second is to realise the potential gains once the transaction is completed.

Studies reveal that when measured by stock-market reactions, mergers and acquisitions on average do create value, but most or all of it accrues to the target firm's owners, and, not surprisingly, the dealers and fixers of the acquisitions.

Getting big also doesn't appear to turn all organisations into angels, either in terms of ethical behaviour, or in terms of generosity to shareholders. BP's attitude to safety standards in the US appeared to have been tainted by a focus on other aspects of the company's agenda, i.e. profit at almost all cost, and duly the reputation of the once idealised Chairman was tainted.

HSBC Bank's actions in the US in the mid 2000s also suggested they may have had eyes on profit bigger than their belly.

GlaxoSmithKlein had merger blues reflected in its share price for years. Scale clearly brings new levels of challenges, in the same way celebrity can act as a negative virus on many individuals. When you employ tens of thousands of people across many time zones, it appears that power and complexity feature prominently in the mind-sets of managers, often apparently further clouding the need for such inconveniences as transparency.

Corporate security can act as a lens to both clarify and focus on transparency in such environments. But in operating cultures where transparency itself is not at or near the top of management's agendas, which would be an interesting measure in its own right, then security's role will be equally diminished. In these worlds, security needs to be pushed harder by outsiders like large institutional investors, who require clarity to serve their own customers interests properly. Even they require the occasional visit to the optometrist (Enron...). And of course the large investors can also have challenges when it comes to transparency and openness.

> ***Security's potential role as a driver of transparency may come as a shock to some people, but we regard its contribution here as one of enhancing the long-term protection of company assets and values.***

This can become very significant when working with acquisitive companies. Research from KPMG and elsewhere indicates that about 65% of acquirers fail to realise their perceived synergy targets.[10]

Intelligence-influenced security has a role to play in support of comments like this:[11]

"Chief executives must pick targets carefully, conduct exhaustive due diligence, and ensure they know enough about what they are buying. Otherwise, disaster will follow". AOL/TimeWarner clearly suffered from 'synergy myopia' in this regard.This is another example of what happens without the input of professional business outset security, the modern expression of the old adage "don't lock the stable doors after the management horses have bolted".

In 2006 Lockheed Martin was forced to walk away from a $2 billion merger with Titan. The collapse of the deal focused on the Foreign Corrupt Practices Act (FCPA) that criminalizes the bribery of foreign officials by US organisations and individuals pursuing business in foreign countries. Titan missed the deal and a fine of over $25 million.[12]

When deadlines loom, a degree of hubris is present, and rewards look high, management teams, who after all are still mostly human, often become over focused on strictly commercial terms, combined sales, synergies, and cost savings, often forgetting or suppressing some key due diligence issues.

"Ethics and compliance failures can be very significant".[13] Even when specialist M&A consultants are involved, corporate security should have a close relationship with all the teams involved.

At the January 2007 World Economic Forum in Davos, the topic of risk was at least an agenda-topping item, which *The Economist* considered originally to be a good sign. However, it also noted that there is a difference between worrying about risk and doing something about it. Some argued that more sophisticated financial markets improved the pricing and distribution of risk[14] and that resilience had increased, while others pointed out that market calmness is like a deceptively still ocean seen from a mountain top, caused by benign but not permanent economic conditions. Warren Buffet said, "It's only when the tide goes out that you learn who's been swimming naked". Who is right? Look at it this way – maybe Warren is a wise Security Leader.

> ***Security's potential role as a driver of transparency may come as a shock to some people, but we regard its contribution here as one of enhancing the long-term protection of company assets and values.***

7. Achieving a Secure Advantage

"Fundamentalists looked back to some simpler and stable and more comprehensible age of the imagined past. It offered an idealistic form of security – escape the present trouble by returning to a non-existent past."[1]

"Our image of corporate perfection is locked in the past – reflected in accounting procedures, management principles, generic strategies, office design, use of language etc. At least the past gave you something to hold onto."[2]

Management teams need to know which critical factors will help keep business competitive in the months and years to come. Knowing what the implications of these factors are has a crucial influence on designing and configuring the business and its supporting organisation. The feasibility and relevance of leading edge security applications and experiences in addressing these factors and challenges is a strategic issue, globally.

We believe all security management applications should emerge from a core strategy. All businesses have different ways of operating, but the essence of a best practice approach to security management conferring a secure advantage is:

The function of security management is to create and maintain a secure condition in which people are safe, the business will flourish, the organisation's reputation will be enhanced, and opportunities for improvements, like with governance, will be identified and acted upon.

In our experience, the building of a successful, sustained security management role cannot be achieved through complex rules and sign-offs.

Our experience also tells us that it is essential to instil in the organisation those beliefs and practices that endorse common sense and trust as critical factors in building value.

The embedding of this approach and attitude towards security management can help achieve world-class standards and benchmarks, especially in relation to good governance criteria. We have worked with the CEOs, Boards, and specialist functional teams in global commercial enterprises whose reputations and other essential assets are being challenged vociferously every day. We have developed ways of helping achieve synergies in operational activities between essential functions.

Here are some more examples of how what we call the Secure Advantage approach works.

In one Eastern European country, some suspicions had arisen about whether a senior manager was defrauding a company. An investigation was conducted with Audit examining all the figures, and Security looking at peripheral circumstances, including the lifestyle of the suspect manager. Accounts were found to be in order. But the manager's lifestyle included ownership of 4–5 houses that appeared to have required funding well above the employee's pay grade, and which he hadn't inherited, married into, or won a lottery for. Security examined major deals done and discovered one for the placing of 600 large posters/placards in the streets. The planned locations were noted and a physical inspection undertaken. Less than 200 of the sites existed. There had been an agreement between the manager and the media operation to use sites, but no due diligence had been conducted.

This is going one step beyond compliance, regulatory or legal due diligence. Security went deeper, further. On a path littered with stones, it didn't just count the number of stones or note whether the stones were legally placed, it lifted each stone to find out was lurking underneath, a discovery process that would appeal to the Stephen Jay Gould or Hercule Poirot in us. This was an attack not only on revenue but on value and reputation, which corporate security was able to tackle.

In another case, retailers were complaining that they were being pushed by a particular wholesaler. The wholesaler would only sell a particular brand if the buyer also agreed to buy bulk beverages from him. These beverages were counterfeited products of famous brands, with an inferior taste. The reputation damage through being linked to inferior products could have been significant, but was identified and stopped at an early stage.

When Corona US beer sales were touching the million cases a month mark, mysterious rumours began circulating that the bright yellow Corona beer actually contained traces of human urine. This proved difficult to quash without calling more attention to it. The rumour was turning out to be very effective, causing an immediate plunge in sales and a crisis mood in the Mexican HQ. The company was obsessively quality-oriented and meticulous about the clarity and purity of its product. The crisis management team was able to track down the source of the rumour to a Nevada distributor of rival beer brands. The parent company, Grupo Modelo, invited lots of journalists to visit the company's modern state-of-the-art breweries, while initiating a legal process against the rumour-mongers, which stopped them. The subsequent positive publicity led to greater demand for the product and ultimately aided efforts to expand into other export markets. In 1997, Corona became America's leading beer import, with 30% of this market segment, some 11 share points ahead of its nearest rival. The company is now exporting to 150 countries.[3]

It doesn't always work out like this in life.

"But in all my experience, I have never been in any accident...of any sort worth speaking about. I have seen but one vessel in distress in all my years at sea. I never saw a wreck and never have been wrecked nor was I ever in any predicament that threatened to end in disaster of any sort." This was a certain E K Smith, 1907, later Captain, *RMS Titanic*.

Things happen relative to your expectations. If your expectation is based solely on things which have happened in the past then you are likely to be in for a surprise tomorrow. As Yogi Berra quipped, "The future ain't what it used to be". Our modes of thinking depend on the context we are in, the domain we are structured within, so we often react to things not based on logic, but on the basis of our surrounding framework, and how that affects our social or emotional systems. Change the domain, or circumstances, and you change the reaction. This is especially true of crisis scenarios.

In a crisis we often over-interpret, and then look for stories which simply encapsulate events for us. This can be doubly deceptive. The need to look at raw data or facts is often then compounded by the need to build explanations around them to 'hold them together'. For many people this adds up to something making sense. It also leads to conspiracy theories, which are often masterful at selection and simplicity. In reality, this process may cloud the ability to see the truth, until someone comes along and reveals the original level of actuality. For example, Niall Ferguson, a historian with an economics background, in his book on the First World War[4] was able to show that despite all the contemporary accounts describing the so-called escalating crisis, war came as a total surprise. This was based on his analysis of imperial bonds which had not declined and which contradicted previous examples of the reaction of investors to anticipating conflicts.

Back in a momentarily sober and crisis-manageable world:

> *Security and shareholder value are entwined in the most successful companies.*

Once you can be assured as much as the world will ever offer up assurances, that security is fulfilling its foundation role as a protector of people and all other essential assets, you can peek at security's capabilities as an enabler of trust, and a deliverer of incremental value across a whole business, wherever you operate.

We believe security, properly managed, can act like a brand, and deliver similar benefits when it is trusted in the same way that the best brands are. This fundamentally links security to the hearts and minds of people, their cultures, and their communities. It repeatedly delivers a promise, and earns respect for that. The best security also has the intrinsic characteristics necessary to meet unthinkable and unexpected challenges. Identifying the potential for crises is only a part of that.

> *Security is about the successful understanding and management of motivations.*

Achieving a Secure Advantage needs to address all these human characteristics as well as any physical or tangible elements.

> *The function of security management is to create and maintain a secure condition in which people are safe, the business will flourish, the organisation's reputation will be enhanced, and opportunities for improvements, like with governance, will be identified and acted upon.*
>
> *Security and shareholder value are entwined in the most successful companies.*
>
> *Security is about the successful understanding and management of motivations.*

---

8. Making Security Make Sense

As with nation states, no effective security management portfolio can successfully operate outside the cultural context of the host. It is essential to become familiar with this critical dimension. The best solutions will only emerge from recognising how this approach and insight will help realise the most effective bespoke fit for a particular environment.

Recognising weaknesses in situations and places that look perfect and safe is neither easy, nor in many cases, welcome. There is a necessity for sensitivity and empathy in challenging structures, systems, and procedures in businesses, organisations, and communities, objectively, and sometimes, confidentially.

Since culture is a function of people, everything hinges on them. Technology and systems are simply there to serve. That being said, it is critical to ensure that the quality of relationships with and between all critical company and country functions can be enhanced through the judicious use of security management technology tools, and also through ideas, attitudes, and behaviour. Security management practices will necessarily look different in organisations and societies whose cultures are different, yet achieving the best fit will yield integrated security benefits of equal robustness.

Here is a dilemma. If every situation looks and feels different, how can anyone be anything other than reactive to them? One of the answers lies in understanding what is really going on at deeper levels, and recognising distractions and distortions from underlying realities. It is essential here to put together teams with the right characteristics that can be trained in intelligence-influenced security practices that will benefit the whole organisation, and be attuned to responding to differences with equally effective results.These characteristics will naturally embrace the ability to 'get under the skin' of an organisation, all the people that have to be dealt with, a society, and its business, in deep and transparent ways. The use of the word *transparency* here will again create a strong reaction in many people who believe that security can only operate on some kind of 'dark-side', as opposed to being the dark matter that holds everything together.

Security can enhance the benefits of transparency.

It's important to stress the need to understand the cultures of the companies and communities being worked with. Many large multi-nationals, for example, take a long time to develop policies, or indeed may be averse to the very word. They are also often averse to sharing things 'until they are right'. In this case, rather than waste time and effort in trying to effect change in a top-down way, it may be better to capitalise on ground-level successes through a judicious communications programme. This can create a sibling rivalry effect, where other business units decide they want to make the same changes. When enough have done this, it is easier to make it a general policy. This is a form of transparency that can speed up progress, but it can also dramatically impede progress in the wrong cultural climate. It may seem obvious, but many people fall foul of not understanding the context of where they are operating.

For every seemingly fresh idea and perspective, there are precedents, variations of long-established behaviours and responses, which can be identified. Through the eyes of intelligent security, greed, corruption, mistrust, dishonesty, selfishness and unwitting errors are just some of the negative things we see in new guises as each society and community shapes itself around rising and falling ethical standards. It is through working to have a deeper understanding of how the behaviour of those around us is driven by religious, social, cultural and economic differences that we are able to identify and separate new forms and fashions from underlying attitudes and behaviour.

By understanding motivations it is possible to design better security management capabilities.

In essence, successful security management cannot be taken out of the core context of people's lives, and the places where they live and work. It is fundamentally a human activity. Security without this context of connectedness is about as useful as trying to choose clothes for someone whose size and gender you don't know anything about. While understanding alone cannot deliver 100% foresight, it does support and enable you to translate insights into substantial risk reduction strategies and sustainable solutions, for a broad spectrum of environments.

We will now look at some of these core contexts and the outcomes and implications they engender.

Between 1989 and 1999 two barriers came down in the world, with profound and continuing consequences. The first was the Berlin Wall, and with it the detritus of the Cold War. The second was the emergence of the mass media download model, and the embryonic upload model for individuals, facilitated by the Internet. The biggest problem for most security operations is that they were often still too attached to tangible aspects of business like bricks and barriers and firewalls, and they played far too small a role in the intangible business of values. Security's role in being able to contribute to these newer forms of differentiating values was under-realised and under-utilised.

The dismantling of the first barrier not only changed the relatively simplistic balance of power in the world that many had got used to, and led to greater fragmentation in world affairs, but it changed our views on what barriers and walls would come to look like, even whether there would be anything to actually see. There were barriers and walls that were also now less physical indicators of separations, though that didn't dampen the enthusiasm of some nations for still erecting them in support of their geographical border issues. Furthermore, ideological symbols, or symbols of differences in ethnicity or faith, have built less permeable but more challenging barriers.

The Internet led to the breakdown of a different kind of barrier. Pre-internet was the view that said you could only reach the masses through expensive broad-scale media distribution, like broadcast media, and print, and large scale producers talking to individuals individually would always remain expensive. Not only that, the view was that people were passive, they were consumers of material and messages.

In the Marshall Plan, which was designed to give post-World War II aid to tired and depleted victors, recipients were forced to import only Hollywood movies. The Internet helped people realise that talking individually to individual others could be done easily and cheaply, as well as effectively. Telecom and media providers held back, which is why they introduced ADSL. The people want downloads, they chanted. Why would they ever want to upload anything, they patronised? People can create their own content, be creative, and distribute it in ways the media seers didn't envisage, and didn't want. The demand to have products and services like 'MySpace', 'YouTube', 'Facebook' etc. hasn't slowed down. Of course, there are many out there who see the rise of the individual as a dangerous form of iconoclasm, and they are building electronic walls and barriers to try to slow down the movement. They live in former Stalin-like worlds where 'truth belongs to the powerful', forgetting that some States and a lot more people have changed, but clearly not everyone.

Some walls have come tumbling down, to be replaced with less visible walls. Other walls have gone up where previously there were none. The wall business is still big business. If you can get your mouth round it, Wall Sreet now meets a whole new world of walls. Security was also used to the old physical walls and barriers. "You're in security – go build a high wall. And guard it." Security was out there. You could see it. You could sense it. For the most part you didn't really like it, but you had to put up with it. Security was, by and large, something done by them, by other people, to us, and it was a kind of speciality you didn't want to get too close too. It was in fact a territory or domain with its own self-protective barriers, full of people who came from specialist backgrounds, knew, or claimed to know, what they were doing, knew each other, and were out of the main circuit, or loop, of the business or organisation they were protecting. They took care of The Boss.

In most organisations, security was nowhere near a core business function, and the head of security wasn't regarded as a senior core business team manager. Often he (since it usually was a he) preferred it this way, and he held members of the organisation he serviced in a kind of benign contempt for their ignorance of what professional security was all about. This led to its own form of exclusivity nurtured and protected by security people who had made the unfortunate decision to deal with non-security professionals in commercial or public environments. Many who had built careers in military or law-enforcement environments considered moving into commercial security as infra dig. This persisted through the nineties, while organisations were building other ways of doing business, internally and externally, reflecting the tearing down of other old physical and intangible barriers.

Several security operations were even more isolated from events in this evolutionary period, showing no real signs of adaptation to new environments and practices. When new barriers had to be built again – the ever present tension between entrepreneurship and protection, there were security people with no competence or connections to provide new forms of protection, which seems somewhat ineffective in a world where there appears to be an innate need to erect walls and barriers, whatever their form. It is also a dangerous situation to be in where a just-in-time globalised economy works wonders when it works, but raises new levels of weakness and uncertainty in the face of adverse conditions.

In the emerging methods of operating, with networks and open operating standards, while there was significant activity going on in what we might call IT Security, an emerging warrior class fighting invisible foes with fancy named weapons, there was often no parallel development of security and competencies to enhance other networked functions, whether they lay in new areas of value creation, or in new areas of compliance and regulation – protection and enabling in tandem.

In a way, security was still piping its tune from the turrets of Martello towers, those prettily sited stone constructions built around the English coastline to provide a form of early warning system about the prospect of a Napoleonic invasion, where each tower was in sight of the next one and could issue a signal, by beacon or fire, to herald warnings of impending attack, while everyone else had dispersed into the fields around.

Security people were literally keepers of the old flame.

Security was too often tolerated and not respected. Security didn't have a seat at the top table. It didn't have the ear of the American audience now known as the 'C-Suite', for example. Security wasn't some place you could build a career, it was a place where people served out time after their first career had been played out elsewhere.

The message was clear. Mr Senior Management might well summarise it all like this:

"Security here is a cost of doing business and should just get on with its limited remit. Security and its people have neither the competences nor the inclination to help define company strategy, goals, and shareholder values. Security is destined to remain the recipient of the leftovers because it doesn't have the means to justify a bigger and better portion. It doesn't look the same, dress the same, or talk the same language. More security is unaffordable and bad for business."

Here's how this kind of perception actually develops:

A major department store in Sweden had experienced tremendous problems with shoplifting. Finally, management decided to do something. They appointed a head of security to take care of the problem. The result – more things disappeared. The reason – by making this issue a big thing for a select few, the others stopped caring.[1]

Security creates barriers. It builds walls. It's "Just Another Brick in the Wall", as Pink Floyd might define it. It's called "You Can't Do That", as another old band, The Beatles, might have captured it.

Someone who understood all that 'no' stuff very well wrote a poem about it – John Cooper Clarke: simply called "Don't".[2] Brilliantly, this ran as the soundtrack to a commercial for a British newspaper, *The Independent*.

For too many people, security is about telling people what they can't do, not what they can do. There's often not enough motivation to care, which is a fabulous opportunity for those who specialise in exploiting these circumstances for their personal advantage. To reprise the point, the biggest problem for many security operations is that they are still too attached to those tangible aspects of business, the bricks and barriers we've described, and play far too small a role in the intangible business of values, knowledge, and intellectual capital. Yet as we can see from an analysis of the way successful companies have developed, value no longer resides alone in physical things.

Emerging value often lies in elements like design, information, IP, service, and image rights. An old-style structure model for corporate security would have looked like this:

Corporate Security Team

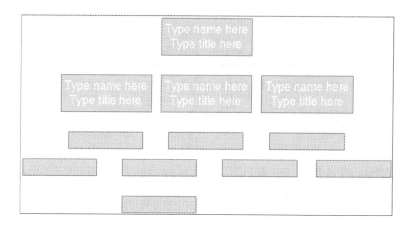

The new world model might look like this:

Business Integrated Security Team

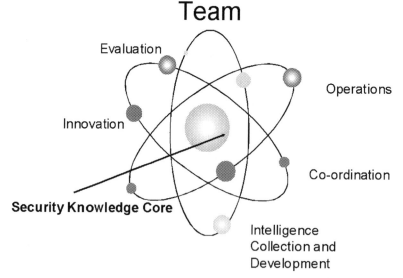

This is much less about organisational structure *per se* than about perspectives on how security might be regarded in an enlightened organisation.

Let's come back to one of our favourite themes – the outset security model:

In the same way that you probably wouldn't start a meeting about Mergers and Acquisitions without one or two experts in the room, or that it would be unusual to have a regional sales meeting without representation from sales and marketing, there should be no meeting started that will have an impact on an enterprise's shareholder value and reputation without a perspective on security. Just what this perspective might reveal depends on the approach to outset security.

Here is an example of how a perspective can be changed:

An ambitious and able regional executive of a large multinational believed he had identified a potential acquisition target that would do two things – help the organisation build a significant regional advantage competitively, and enhance his promotional prospects to the company board.

The board also thought they had recognised the significance of the opportunity, and a process of due diligence began, yet with a strong determination to proceed to a deal. In the later stages of the expensive and rapid due diligence process, security was 'by invitation', asked to take a cursory look at the target company and its directors.

Security due diligence revealed that had the deal proceeded at that stage, the revelation of the practices of the directors and previous behaviour of the acquisition target would have rapidly led to serious value and reputation issues for the acquiring company as a whole. The deal was called off. The regional director suffered no career limitation, and the acquiring company proceeded along other paths. The target company's business subsequently collapsed.

The automatic application of an outset security mindset would have saved money, time, and resource, at a manageable point of the M&A strategy execution, without having to become involved in a major due diligence exercise, and with little loss of face for anyone involved.

A multinational company making a major investment in Russia in the early '90's involved the purchase of an existing Russian production company, a market leader. The project team had conducted what it considered to be a normal and thorough due diligence process – accounts, legal, compliance, market analysis etc, and had also been represented by leading consulting specialists in all these areas. All looked good, a price had been agreed. And then the acquiring company's project team was issued with a threat ...

Millions of dollars having been expended already; at this late stage the deal looked as though it would have to be brought to an embarrassing halt. The nature of the threat was that project team members' lives would be at risk if the Western company, on securing ownership of the Russian asset, did not agree to use one named bank and one named distribution company exclusively for the whole of the Russian Federation. The threats were delivered by the senior Russian representative of one of the world's largest merchant banks. The corporate security department of the Western company was knowledgeable about the proposed acquisition but had not been closely involved in conducting background due diligence on all participants.

The threatened, extremely frightened and worried project team leader phoned the global chief security officer, who immediately requested their return to the West, and organised a team to take stock of the situation. At the first action meeting, Western representatives of the merchant bank concerned were invited to attend. In the meantime the chief security officer and his team had now conducted effective due diligence on the niche operations of the Russian bank subsidiary and the distribution company who would have been the beneficiaries of this criminal pressure.

It was evident that both serious organised crime and high-level political connections were instrumental in the threats. At the meeting, attended by the project team and representatives from the merchant bank, it became clear that precious little knowledge of the background of the senior Russian 'representative' existed. He had been deemed to be "a super chap", who spoke wonderfully fluent English and "was most relaxed in social circumstances". Even at this stage the Western representatives of the bank found it hard to believe that their Russian man could be involved in such criminality. The resolution of the situation was led by the chief security officer.

At that time in Russia, some of the biggest Russian companies, especially banks, had their interests safeguarded by large protection forces, not unlike private militia. The chief security officer arranged for the bank's Russian representative to be informed that the company would not succumb to the threats, that any incidents or manifestations of the threats would be escalated into an international scandal, and that, in any case, for its banking and distribution needs the company was already negotiating with two other named banks and distribution companies, all of which were known to have equal or larger protection capability than those in the threat scenario. The goal of the tactic was to dissuade the perpetrators from continuing with their threats while allowing the project to move on towards a successful conclusion, without the impediment of other embarrassments.

The bank's Russian representative was duly informed.

About three weeks later in a Western capital at a meeting to celebrate the success of the acquisition, a different very senior Russian representative in the negotiating process informed the business development director of the Western company that he was aware of the threat that had been issued, and that the situation had been defused. He gave a personal assurance that the company would never again be threatened in such a manner. The Russian subsidiary, now acquired, went on to be one of the most important successes in the operations of the global operation.

The lessons are that you don't solve dangerous problems without security, or with a crude security approach. The earlier involvement of security due diligence, i.e. outset security, looking into the backgrounds of key participating entities could have helped avoid the threat occurrence, or certainly helped the project team be more ready and able to deal with it if it had occurred. A Secure Advantage would have been achieved earlier. Any assumption that the situation at that time in Russia could have been resolved by the law enforcement agencies alone would not have got to a result. Had the Western company terminated its acquisition at the time of the threat, its overall sacrifice in acquisition costs would have been about $140 million in the early 1990s. The new corporate security-derived solution involved imagination, innovation, and the ability to think and act laterally.

But to be involved from the start requires characteristics other than those of a sleuth to receive the invitation to be the driver of outset security.

If you are already a security specialist, use the next chapter as a chance to review how the role you play is evolving. Whoever you are, observer or investor, you will see that the only way forward is through the closer integration of security with the organisation's overall goals and objectives. That way it may have been able to help the following character:

A banker visited a Latin country and found the government officials charming and intelligent – sounds familiar? He had been entertained at a country club, with French food and wine, and he had gone to a race meeting which was described as very civilised. During this fact-finding visit of 48 hours he had formed a very favourable impression of the country. This was the basis for recommending the loan of billions of dollars to the country, which could not and would never pay back. There were probably multiple agendas at play, but one of them wasn't that from security pointing out the possible lack of solidity in this assessment of the robustness of the investment proposal.

Does the version of a secure environment, from your perspective, look the same as it does to others around you? It's worth reflecting that each generation is driven by unique ideas about security. That means that the different generational experiences and values of those around us shape our needs, so unless you are in an environment where you are only surrounded by your peer organisation, it becomes important to understand that the motives of each generation can also be used to help make approaches to developing a successful security strategy more effective.

As a new security leader gets appointed and celebrates the event, it may be a time for some when 15–20 years of successful career building and experience is at its peak. That experience may well come from other kinds of organisations and environments. Sometimes, also, without recognising it, the age and maturity brought to the post also has a trail behind it called youth and attitude. The person, traditionally, may be more senior (in years) than others holding similar ranks. This also has an affect on perspective and perceptions. There are already a couple of generations looking to the time when that newly taken seat or function will be theirs, and on the evolution goes. What kind of position has been taken up, and what influence will it really bring to bear, in the context of the influence of previous experience?

"The common experiences of a generation create a specific sensibility that touches each of its members in some way – what's funny, what's stylish, what's taboo, what works and what doesn't, what to aspire to and what to avoid."[3]

We share life experiences from our formative years. Beyond any specific current organisation culture we happen to find ourselves in, we unconsciously embrace the culture we were borne in to, the economic conditions of our society, world events, natural disasters, heroes and villains, politics, communication and technology. These experiences link groups of people together into units the sociologists call cohorts. As a consequence of this kind of organising, how we manage and trade our world-views, or 'schemata', is significant.

Walking into the new security leader role, the wise manager will have access to the demographics and psychographics of people in the organisation, and should now also be in a position to take a generational snapshot of who is there to help get a deeper understanding of the way each influential generation is impacting on the organisation.

The generations can be designated like this for now:

- Matures   born between 1909–1945
- Baby Boomers   1946–1964
- Generation "X"   1965–1985
- Generation "Y"   1986–now
- Generation "Z"   1990–now

Segmentation is a fascinating subject, because there is always a bias in it. Much time, especially in marketing and sales disciplines, is spent on determining the nuances between sub-segments of teenage and young adult markets. Remember how old someone seemed when he was in a class two years above you? No-one thinks of the young as a homogenous organisation.

It also seems much sexier to push the emotional buttons of the first half of life. So, at the over 50's level, they are often dismissed en masse as wrinklies or past it – that's them folks, not us of course… Today's marketers are neglecting the actual nuances and subtleties of a third or more of many Western populations, and furthermore it's often the third with money to invest and the time to make considered decisions. Increasingly, segmentations will get more subtle as we move towards the autumnal zones, and we will have to acknowledge young olds and old olds. Oddly, it's not so different from noticing when we were teens that some of our peers actually seemed to want to be middle-aged even then, but we are less forgiving of those than of the ones who want to be forever young. Each individual in these shifting sands will have different needs and expectations from security.

And in today's world, they may be our boss for years to come. So reconsider the oldsters and realise that they may be willing to try new brands and experiences, concealing as many differences in attitudes and make-up as the rest of the segmented population. But then you revert to type and say, "I never understood my parents, and they don't understand me."

When you are in Brasil, or Iraq, with predominantly young populations today, the entire set of attitudes towards society and security might be significantly different. Equally, cultural differences, like between family oriented eastern markets, and the pursuit of individualism of the young in many Western societies, drives major differences in perceptions and behaviour.

Consider generational drivers for different groups.

Moving from the philosophical to the profitable, the key learning here is that the short sighted application of the values and attitudes simply of our own generation, to the development of security strategies for another generation, and culture, both in society and in organisations, can perpetuate misunderstanding and lead to commercial failure. Making security make sense requires a keen ability to manage multiple perspectives, and to communicate with a strong empathy with different groups, mind-sets, and culture.

New security policies for new generations would benefit from learning from the past, especially when most of the time people think that only the present is the time we know best about everything. So we should look to a world where introductions must succeed through empathy and simplicity. There needs to be acceptable functionality, not over-engineered 'look at all we can do' functionality. Conflict points for the coming generations are:

"What I get" – *not* – "What it's got."

For governments and corporations, it's about reconciling – "What we give you" – not -"What you want".

Security and its management will have to come to terms with resolving the paradox that its services will increasingly be subject to this kind of scrutiny, and that while security will continue to depend on technology, it will also make a difference by understanding better how its representation of values affects different observers and their place and perspective in demographic and generational terms. In terms of communicating security news to the generations, a snapshot might look like this

For...

- Matures   Summarise it   Revolutionary
- Boomers   Organise it   Novel
- "X"ers   Open it   Interesting
- "Y"s   "You tell me..."   Maybe...
- "Z"s   "I'll tell you,,," Listen again

That's probably more than the current range of styles many security teams are utilising today. The way forward lies partly then in looking back, to understanding generations' needs, wants, and likely responses. This means being tough enough to know as much about why we might not be succeeding with some organisations as why we are with others. Finding cross-generational bridges is clearly important as well.

Businesses and brands need to be introducing themselves to new people all the time. This means flexible communication approaches and a deeper understanding of the values driving all those we are likely to be connected with. If security can be regarded as a brand with brand values then it needs to behave in the same way. This is an affirmation about secure protection and enablement being a value-driven business.

The old security leader was a master of building barriers.

The new security leader needs to be a master of building bridges, an engineer of trust.

Here is an example of just this kind of excellence from one of the world's most successful retail businesses:

H was recruited for the post of Head of Loss Prevention and Security in one of the key Asian markets. H was a major in the Army and came to them knowing nothing about retail. He was the first person to hold this post in the country (the business was new). He came to the company for an induction programme with the security team and it was obvious from the outset that he had huge potential.

When the business was set up Security lacked any credibility and was seen as existing outside the core business. H by sheer hard work and force of personality changed all that and ensured that the function really added to the bottom line and his team were totally integrated into the business. Within a year or two he was promoted. He was then sponsored for a job as Director responsible for Supply Chain. He devoured that task. He opened one of the largest warehouses in the world and brought credit not only to himself but also to the Security function.

He is now the retail director for all small store formats in that country and his side of the business is leading the rest of the functions in terms of profitability.

This is a real success story that demonstrates how important it is to integrate the security function into the core business and to have individuals who can cross over functions and make it work. He also has a superb grasp of cultural needs and generational drivers.

This is bridge building at its best.

Security can enhance the benefits of transparency.

By understanding motivations it is possible to design better security management capabilities.

The new security leader needs to be a master of building bridges, an engineer of trust.

---

9. Security Leadership

In this chapter we concentrate on who might best demonstrate the most rounded set of skills to enable security to deliver more value. Here we launch a series of views and projections about what the future security leader or team may look like, where he or she or they might come from, and what they will be expected to do.

What are the required characteristics of the new security leader and leadership?

Here are three thoughts to get debate off the ground:

- The only thing that we can trust is that what is certain becomes the uncertain and the unlikely becomes likely.
- The three drivers moving us forward into the unknown are changes in technology, institutions, and values.
- Beware of saying "Everything is security".

The established security leader should feel familiarity with the concept in the first quotation. In the second, there are fewer people who are masters of all the details in changes logged as drivers. You could argue that no one can stay on top of everything, but that is what is expected of those we invest with leadership roles. Yet even here we are on dangerous ground, since qualities of leadership, and expectations about the fruits of leadership, are simultaneously changing. In the third, we steer clear of the tendency to try to see things only with one pair of eyes

Let's look at the technology drivers of change first. Eric Hobsbawm[1] writes about technology revolutionising the arts by making them omnipresent. The role of the radio, its later enabling transistor, TV, and video cassette players, all are catalogued as transformers of perception, yet there is no mention of the mobile phone, DVD players, or the Internet. How could there be? Even though they were around, there had yet to be a true explosion of uptake – it was, after all, 1994.

Bangalore is now the world's second largest city for software development. Who would have put money on that fact 15 years ago? Or that in India, the "Zippies" out of the emerging generation Z, are some 550 million people between 15 and 25 years old, all wanting to get the most out of new technology to help them get the most out of life.

The burgeoning availability of media tools and people to use them has created enormous challenges for security leaders both to meet the demands of employers wishing to have access to their people, customers, and suppliers, and also to protect the tangible and intangible assets entangled with the technologies. Let's face it, a security leader today is likely to have more specialist knowledge about certain aspects of security than others, but is unlikely to have specialist knowledge about everything. How do you resolve the dilemma between expectation and capability?

It is clear that to stay ahead today requires a dependence on others. Co-operation is the key to providing a world-class service. Building the right team to service ever changing organisations trying to match or exceed market rates of change has become more significant than ever. Security cannot be like T S Eliot's "still point in a turning world"[2]. It needs to be elastic.

Let's take the second drivers of change – Institutions. We claim institutions are structures we create to promote stability and predictability. This is meant to reduce uncertainty. But institutions are like chimaeras. They shift and evolve to ensure their survival. And the institution of responses to change grows and shifts by the day as well. The current trend in reducing uncertainty is to cover every available surface with words. In the days when lawyers and clerks were paid by the word, documents, unsurprisingly, got longer. Maybe the same holds true today. Look what we've got. The *Declaration of Independence* contained only four pages in its original form, yet the manual for a basic printer now runs to 50 pages, and the latest EU pronouncement on the growth, marketing, sales and distribution of cabbages, runs to over 2000 pages. Literary Mann Booker Prize hopefuls probably don't need to lose sleep over this.

Sadly, words alone cannot prevent people from doing things, but they can slow down the rate at which things can be done, simply by taking up more of people's time to absorb what they are going on about. Accounting practices have not been slow to realise the commercial benefits of this trend, as they have moved to advise their clients on how to handle ever more complex demands about disclosure, compliance, and 'proper' governance.

A security leader in a dynamic organisation should be in a position to contribute to the effective management of these kinds of new demands and developments across the whole organisational base. This means being able to create a point of view, a perspective, and a position that will be respected and expected from other senior cross-functional heads, including those in areas like audit, treasury, risk management, legal, sales, and marketing.

A well-assembled case on objectivity with regard to compliance, from a security perspective, should be something any director or senior management person would feel compelled to look at, not simply because of the legal obligation to observe good practice, but because of the impact on the business, values, and reputation of the organisation.

This leads us on to the third driver of change – values. Our values are also being challenged every day. As well as the regular series of attacks on societal values, which in themselves vary immensely, there are attacks on organisational values not only from disaffected outsiders, but also from those inside organisations whose less than transparent endeavours in the pursuit of personal shareholder value gave us such delightful news stories as the aforementioned Enron, Tyco, WorldCom, and Parmalat, for starters, and that's before we mention certain financial services specialists.

Let us not forget that the leaders of these kinds of organisations were for years lauded by the media and by business associates and partners as exemplars of a particularly egotistical and charismatic – read desirable while the money looked like it was coming in – form of leadership. Meanwhile, in corridors of academia, a different set of researchers were noting the long-term success of companies whose leaders were rather quieter, who had a long-term view of company development, and who were far less interesting for the media to profile at the time. The leaders who were tempted to fly too high left far more damaging legacies than the unaffected care to think. That's the point. Acts of terrorism appear to find their way into our collective consciousness time and time again. But if you were closely connected to Enron, or Arthur Andersen, or Lehman Bros, other people's consciousness of the damage, the destruction, and the suffering, diminishes rapidly in the face of more long-running media-nurtured tales of terrorism or other attention grabbing disasters. Several former Western companies championed as gold-star performers in democratic capitalism have damaged far more people directly than terrorists.

Whether values are being tested by religious malcontents or greedy suits, security leaders need to be in a position to declare and uphold value systems, and to get better at recognising and responding to a value system that is becoming corrupted. This is a major call on objectivity and personal strengths, resilience, and commitment, which we acknowledge has been too challenging for some people to subscribe to. Whistleblowers have not been subject to a history of garlanded praise any time recently.

Even spotting a gap between professed ethical practice and performance is not possible if a security leader is in no position to observe other leaders closely, and has no voice among them. The security player who is out of the loop may also tacitly accept examples of highly questionable activity in organisations where rewards are high and constraints few. This is not to say that security leaders should be primary custodians of company morality, yet where identified behaviour will have a clear negative impact on company value, the security leader should have the obligation and the voice to point out the implications of actions, while retaining the option to opt out. He or she should be a prime reference point for the dangers of exposure called moral hazard, but without any religious overtones.

But if this person is to have a meaningful voice, more has to be done both to champion security's emergent role and potential as an enabler of trust and enhanced value, and to find people who can best deliver these through that role and route. In some ways, the senior security player should be paid by a trusted third party to lessen the pain of the consequences of pointing out harsh truths.

As with all the other change drivers, there are going to be leaders who can change and adapt, and others who can't, or won't. The ones who are inflexible are unlikely to be able to influence others to change.

So what should an organisation be looking for in its next generation of security leaders? One of the new factors in the modern world that raises the potential importance of a good CSO is the escalation of uncertainty that followed both the relative stability of the Cold War, and the enormous speed at which non-military events now have a global impact today in many areas. Risk intelligence and risk assessment in these times are also more likely to be proved right or wrong during the tenure of the assessor. There are fewer hiding places.

Let's take a look at who's out there right now, and what's coming their way. Once again, you can judge this from the position of a security specialist, as a senior manager, as a value seeker, a shareholder, or as a blend of these. There are fresh perspectives and values whatever the observation point, and here we have created eleven such observation points:

- **Observation Point One**

If you already work in a senior capacity in corporate security, you may have until recently worked in a different world. If your career began and developed in other security environments, from the armed forces to law enforcement agencies, and you elect, or are invited to work in corporate security, there are challenges in three fundamental areas:

- The world you left will still be significantly more familiar than the world you are entering.

- The environment you are entering contains a new amount of significant unknowns from culture to language to values.

- The chances of security management being seen as a business enabler will not emerge unless you are adopted as a co-leader by the host environment.

A number of people will look at this and say that confirms why they decided not to get into the commercial world, or out of the stream of their former speciality. Entering the world of profitable security is not for everyone's tastes or talents.

But if you do enter a new corporate environment, you cannot counter challenges from outside the corporate compound. It is vital to know more about the lifeblood of the organisation, who its people and its customers and its clients are, intimately. How else can relevant solutions be developed? It is not possible to truly develop insightful security practices out of debates about products and services you and your colleagues rarely touch, and for customers you rarely or never meet.

As the Harvard Strategy and Human Resources expert Henry Mintzberg observed,[3] the world is full of people who have been put into leadership positions with little management experience. What is the effect of putting a leader from one place into another place with no appreciation of the organisation's history, and no sense of its culture? What is the effect of imposing a detached outsider on committed insiders?

Security management needs to be in a different place. For instance, seeing oneself as a well-connected node in an organisational network, rather than as a specialist adjunct to it, changes the perception of the role and the service provided.

In a world-class security network, authority for making decisions and developing strategic initiatives has to be distributed, so that responsibility can flow to those best able to deal with the issues at hand. The organisation needs distributed quality intelligence, not security department totemic worship. Who will be best suited to lead in this environment? These questions apply equally to the need for adapted approaches to management in general in enlightened companies. Let's test the proposition further.

- **Observation Point Two**

"Who's trying to spoil my comfort zone?"

We constantly refer to the world we are talking about as being full of gaps between perceptions and reality. This is also true when it comes to questions of skill transferability. Many ex-military, intelligence, and security services people have immense management experience, yet this is often not recognised as such, and it is also often not 'allowed' to be used in different kinds of organisational environments.

In many countries there is an implicit assumption that the military, or military experience, has little connectivity to the business world, despite the latter borrowing heavily from its language in terms of strategy, targeting, logistics' competence, and so on.

A recently retired major general was made CSO of a large insurance organisation. He was a broadly experienced army officer who had had many management functions. When he had been at the insurance company for about six months he overheard the CEO bemoaning the fact that they had been unsuccessful for the second time in acquiring a new director of human resources, and this at a critical stage in the early planning of a major merger. The major general, not being one lacking in confidence, told the CEO with a smile that he need look no further, and explained that he had managed HR extensively and at all levels in his military service. He added he felt sure he could be as effective in the insurance industry as he had been in the armed forces. The CEO, somewhat shocked, said to the major general that it seemed inconceivable that his suggestion could be viable. There was a pause. Of about three months.

Later on, the major general, who combined his skills with considerable charisma, actually won over the CEO. He was given the HR role in addition to his continuing security role and he became very successful in both appointments, leading the HR contribution to the successful planned merger some two years after his appointment.

Don't always judge a book by its covers.

Many of today's CSOs would regard themselves as being at the peak of their careers, or their second careers at the top of their game. Many are. Interestingly, many are a generation older than other stars in the management firmament. Delivering consistently, they might say there were few areas in the organisation where the security service provided wasn't 'making the metrics', especially if they happened to have an American accent. This is all well and good until someone comes along and says, "I see what you're doing but you haven't got the whole picture."

What is the CSO reaction going to be? It depends who has been given the CSO role. One form might sound like this: "Who are these people? Do I want to know them? What can I do about them?"

- **Observation Point Three**

Security's role in leading organisations has changed as significantly over the last ten years as the other drivers of change we noted have, and the rate of change will continue in the next decade. Some of the changes have been introduced by professional security practitioners. But we see more input coming from outside the current boundaries of the security function. These come from people who will make demands on security that have rarely been made before, and they will be accompanied by levels of expectation that will also be new. The focus on business continuity and crisis management in the wake of human criminal attacks or natural disasters has created a new swathe of interested parties in security's arena. The reality is that this is already happening in a number of world-class organisations, and is likely to spread through companies and geographies, large and small. The challenges for security leaders will grow as the role extends, and for those who want to rise to the challenge there will be significant career opportunities for CSOs, or leaders of the security function, established and new, to play a larger role in the way organisations are expected to deliver increased value.

Let's look at other ways in which new demands will be generated. We will show how the perspective for security's role will stretch, and look at how security can satisfy the new demands made on it. As the core expectations of security's contribution to protecting a company's assets come to be regarded as a given, emphasis will shift further to asking of security:

"How is security enhancing and enabling my business?"

The pressure to address this comes almost always from parties beyond the security function. Why should this be so?

Companies and their managements have seen an ever-growing demand from shareholders, stakeholders, the media, and other influencers, to demonstrate that they are delivering value. What this value comprises has also expanded over the last decade, embracing not just more rigorous methods of measuring and accounting for value, but incorporating responses to issues under the banner of corporate social responsibility or ethical policy. As shareholders' thirst for value refuses to be slaked, managements have had to find ways to identify and extract added value from existing resources as well as new markets and products and services.

In this quest for value, no part of the organisation appears to be missed by scrutinising eyes. But we know from experience that scrutiny often finds only what it expects to see, unless it has been further sharpened by the ability to identify and then realise fresh insights from previously unseen potential. This higher level of seeing requires a change of perspective, an openness of mind, and a willingness to try something different, things that in themselves are also not always easy to achieve, especially if they are not simply a reaction to a clear and present threat.

But it can be done. Look at how companies overturned 'the way things are done around here' to build significantly successful and sustained businesses. Remember the time when everything was controlled, owned, and operated inside an organisation? Try telling that to Dell, or Nike, or car manufacturers. Remember when intellectual property was a dull world of patent analysis and file protection? Try telling that to the music and film industries, or the image rights management companies of famous sports stars. Value release requires seeing established things in new ways, and then embracing the change.

- **Observation Point Four**

In the search for incremental value, smart organisations are already looking at the ubiquitous function of security in their operations, and asking a fundamental question:

"Can I get more Value from Security in this business?"

Just as explorers, drillers, and diggers find new ways to tap sources of value, CSOs are beginning to have the opportunity, as well as the obligation, to look at the business of security as an enabling tool, as well as an asset protection function. Where most other strategically essential functions are reaching peaks on value delivery curves, managements are being driven to look at areas where they hadn't made the value 'ask' before. Security is one of the few essential functions remaining that isn't at the value peak, and so represents a rich seam of potential.

To begin to achieve headway in this area, some pre-conditions must be identified and met:

- The starting point is to understand and accept that the most profitable security strategy will emerge not from a ring-fenced security function, but from networked coalitions, including other senior management and cross-functional organisations.

- Coalition members will need to share a common language to determine what precisely an added value security function can deliver in their specific operation.

- As previously distinct functions begin to form one collaborative ring, fresh competences will have to be developed both by the seekers of value, and the deliverers of it.

- Coalitions for delivering an intelligence-influenced integrated business security function must find their support in a willing board, and in security leaders who also believe that security's enhanced role, and their own, will reap fresh rewards.

It is the same for any function seeking to capture time and attention for what new value it may be capable of bringing to the organisation. This was true of embryonic IT functions 20 years ago, of compliance and risk functions, of marketing departments, of almost any function in a Darwinian enterprise over its evolutionary development.

A measure of significant progress is being made when these same organisations of people have reached a positive consensus about the following three critical questions:

1. Do you see security as a business enabler?
2. Do you see security as a core business function?
3. Do you see security as a profit enhancer?

If the answer to any of these questions is 'No', then you are missing out on valuable opportunities.

A CSO today may be in a position where their voice is a lone one with regard to these questions, but that position will change. In the coming years the lone voice will grow into a chorus, as the questions will form in the mouths of the CEO, the "C- Suite", the head of audit or risk, legal or IT, the heads of innovation, and marketing and sales, many of whose functions continue to evolve as they seek answers to the very same questions about their own functions. Claims will be made on security's former 'territories'. Know that the embedding of security in every function is a worthy goal. Ownership should be universal. There are still plenty of things for the security leader to do when this cultural shift has occurred. Success does not have redundancy and obsolescence built into it.

Whoever recognises the opportunity, it will take a coalition to get to 'Yes', and in the meantime, there must be no detriment to any of security's current protective capabilities.

- **Observation Point Five**

The current is moving towards a new form of security leader, like it or not. Those other value drivers and seekers of the time, universities and business schools, are also beginning to market the next change driver – "Uncertainty". For example, 'Managing in an Unpredictable World',[4] was the title of a 5-day strategy programme at the London Business School, 'providing a holistic framework to help management executives and companies succeed in unpredictable markets'. Security can be a key player in building business resilience in an uncertain world.

It is harder to find people who have had more experience with unpredictability than highly experienced security people. They are used to dealing not only with internal threats, but also with external threats that challenge the specific comfort zones of most other people. In bringing imagination to projecting the unthinkable and its consequences, the best practitioners live more easily with the uncertain and the unpredictable, which many people are not comfortable trying to manage.

Although some CSOs may not have the skills to take complex products and projects from pure research, or have the full set of skills to market those applications directly themselves, the understanding of how security principles can help organisations proceed successfully in a provisional world is of immense strategic significance and value, and needs to be marketed appropriately. This conjunction requires respectful teamwork.

What has been missing for most, so far, are the conditions for discovering new potential, and the collaborative means to combine knowledge and skills to release incremental value.

Before anyone wriggles in their 'E-Z' chair and says this is all peripheral to the core job, let's just make a note of something. In those places where the successful delivery of an added value security function has been managed, it has also ensured maximum efficiency and performance for the company in their most exposed areas, including those that deliver the core competence of asset protection. Going down this new direction reinforces foundations as well as innovations.

- **Observation Point Six**

Of course, as each enterprise varies by product, service, structure, and culture, we note again – how the end result looks to observers will vary across markets and geography, but it will be equalised in benchmarking scores for efficiency.

This approach helps see beyond established boundaries. For instance, a look at warehousing protection for a company operating in the Middle East led to innovations in distribution logistics, improved competitive market share, and a more motivated workforce who felt they could be more productive in their enhanced working environment. This could not have happened in a situation where security simply tightened up access procedures to the warehouse and stopped there.

For now, it may be possible to maintain control of an area of expertise, but we suggest the need to formulate answers to the coming questions:

- "Hey, Larry, how am I going to get more value out of your resources next year?"
- "Well, Bob, how are we going to make the numbers this year?"

Try extending the definition of what the company's strengths are, and how as a security leader, they should be seen. By integrating specialist knowledge and roles with a wider coalition, there may be new leadership opportunities, by heading cross function, or multi-functional organisations, not just single functions, to deliver increased shareholder value.

It is much harder to do this if a CSO is conceptually and physically on the periphery of the organisation. Views on how security can enhance the company's strengths, as well as protect its assets, should find willing ears. After all, those very same people have to answer the same question for the whole organisation.

Learning is, in one sense, the ability to develop a fresh perspective. Returning to the business schools for a moment, they are fashioning fresh perspectives about management challenges and leadership. Gone are the God-like images of the purple-cloaked omniscient deliverer, and incoming are the grittier portraits, like this one from Professor Donald Sull of Harvard. "The reality today for many senior managers is to be more like a racing driver on a foggy day, on a fast course, with the competition on their back wheel."[5] The reality is, it's very difficult to see into the future, but we must all still act. As security leaders, experience can play a key part in helping other managers succeed in unpredictable markets, through the application of proven tradecraft from specialist disciplines, adapted to the new operating culture and environment. Accepting this position can enable adaptable CSOs to reconsider security's role, reach and capabilities in supporting the company, and their own personal goals and objectives.

- **Observation Point Seven**

It may be seen as radical to think that the CSO is in a position to demonstrate real potential to reinforce a company's truly competitive position. But this is neither an impossible perspective nor an impossible piece of learning. It has been done.

It has been said[6] that the media industry has not been at the forefront of adapting to the security implications of global terrorism. In one multinational media company, after terrorist attacks in Casablanca, a popular filming location, the security department involved itself in understanding the security and business continuity issues concerned in making films in developing countries. The department created a comprehensive template to cover the whole filming process from the initial selection of locations through the protection of the stars, personnel and assets while filming, to the protection of the intellectual property of the raw product through editing, finishing and showing to test audiences. This template was used to demonstrate to insurance companies and agents that the company took security seriously, leading to reduced premiums and clinching deals with first-choice actors.

A CSO integrated in a large multinational was involved in the process of looking, with other senior management members, at regional business plans. One region's plan was immaculately presented, the numbers looked good, the metrics looked sensible, projections looked ambitious but achievable. The only snag, as the regional director was later to concede, was that in one of the world's most turbulent regions, nothing had been factored into the plan to take account of political or terrorist activity or threats, including the outbreak of war, and the myriad changes these might bring. The plan was out of context and lacked any contingency planning to minimise threat outcomes. This was not a case of arrogance, it was a case of ignorance.

The CEO says he wants 20% 'more' next year so everyone tries to make the numbers. In an oil company, factoring in the danger elements from political or terrorist activity is normal – it's in the culture. For other kinds of companies it is not routine, yet the not routine is becoming more present in global markets, and there is a need for someone to give advice to help planning be more robust – a trusted advisor.

- **Observation Point Eight**

To help, consider security's role as a profitable beacon of trust. Imagine yourself for a moment as part of an enhanced security team, and redefine:

- Who you are today
- Where you are going
- What you stand for
- How you fit in
- How you deliver.

This is as much about attitudes as it is about attributes. After trying that, a security leader will be in a better position to understand how to address the following challenges:

How do you:

- Get more from the same or less next time around?
- Demonstrate value delivery?
- Enhance revenue potential?

- **Observation Point Nine**

The time will come, sooner rather than later, when organisations will have to answer a further question, which is:

- "Who can and should audit the security function?"

This is only one level of detail down from the big questions about audit objectivity and conflicts of interest that are being asked about The Big Four, and which we briefly visited earlier.

Business continuity and resilience management have become core security functions in some leading organisations. The knowledge and experience from those is now ripe for transfer to other domains, and business integrated security has a vital role to play in all these larger scenarios, provided it can pass the same rigorous steps in demonstrating integrity and contribution. Further, as security takes on a vanguard role, it can play a key role in shifting perspectives about the very functions it currently supports.

- **Observation Point Ten**

Cross-functional skills and teams should see the emerging security leader as an equal partner in a collaborative ring. In the end, security leaders have two clearly defined roles:

- How can you simplify the organisation's ability to manage challenges that affect its core values?

- How can you contribute to the organisation's ability to manage challenges that affect its core values?

In the emerging world, world-class security will recognise the scope of this expanded role, and will help drive the security profession to supporting security's evolving role as an enabling tool.

But how does one find one of these new security leaders?

Let's take a generic-type recruitment advertisement for a CSO.

"We are looking for a candidate to take global responsibility for managing security policy and business security planning. The ideal candidate will have solid knowledge and experience in managing security policy within a large organisation. He or she will be able to manage change to reflect best practice and provide assurance of compliance. The post holder will enjoy operating at a senior management level and will commission and manage advice in all aspect of physical and personal security and business continuity worldwide. The successful candidate will have a demonstrable and successful track record in managing protective security in a customer-facing service environment and will be experienced in the technical and procedural requirements of current best practice in security."

...and a generalised job description, or specification, for a CSO:

Role Statement

"To ensure that world-class protective security and security intelligence advice and assistance is provided to all elements of the Company so that threats to its assets and to business operations and activities are properly identified, assessed and countered in a cost effective manner."

Experience Required

"General managerial capabilities. Broad knowledge of the Security Spectrum. Wide range of high level intelligence and security contacts. Experience at working to Board level in a national or international intelligence/security agency – with international/global orientation".

What do you notice about them?

They are basically replete with craft skill requirements, evidence of certificates of achievement, and impressive collections of previous experience borne out of the esteemed operations and environments the candidate has so far operated in. There is significantly less about the personality and un-teachable skills required to operate in a specifically different culture. Some would argue that this element of the recruitment process would clearly be subject to HR assessment and all the other things that happen once an invitation to a formal interview process has been extended. That may well be the case, but mistakes are being made all the time because of a gap between functional competence and leadership 'fit' in a specific corporate culture. There is also the issue of corporate cultures and their effects on organisations. Let's look at this more closely:

A major UK bank wanted a more integrated and intelligence-influenced approach to security. The Board decided to recruit someone they thought could deliver this. They recruited a candidate with eminent military and private security experience and gave him his goals. But within the company culture the Board failed to disseminate and convince its workforce of its intentions to make the changes it desired. At every single place and point the CSO was blocked from making progress. The company had a vision but the nature of the culture rendered the vision impossible to achieve.

By contrast, another multinational bank had the same vision and wanted to do away with its previous corporate cop approach to security. It recruited another highly suitable individual into the CSO role, and with great determination ensured that every part of its organisation understood the Board's intent and its rationale. The first bank continues to have dissonance in its security affairs and procedures, the second has enhanced its capability enormously.

Take an example from a major US financial services operation. They selected a candidate to be a CSO whose functional credentials looked immaculate. He was hired. He was fired four months later. He didn't fit in with the culture. On closer inspection, other CSOs who had known him suggested to the hirers that he didn't have the right profile for the intended role, but the warnings were not heeded. The company lost time and money and had to start the recruitment programme again. The candidate was out in the marketplace without a job. Where did it all go wrong? Fundamentally, not enough time was spent establishing whether the candidate could in reality serve their operating culture and style. It was a question of intangible asset value and fit that they chose not to examine.

In another case, a person was hired to fulfil a senior due diligence role on a compensation package of around $350,000 at the time. After a relatively short period, the appointee was fired. It transpired that the person had in fact never performed an equivalent role before, and had been fired from the most recent previous assignment that had commanded a total compensation package of some $50,000.

It may seem obvious, but it is necessary to re-state that people need to be hired who have the right attitude and behaviour to fit the organisation first, supplemented by their craft skills, and not the other way round. It also helps if some form of responsible due diligence is undertaken, since 'social engineering' specialists can often deliver brilliantly on the first part of the performance assessments, especially where the recruiting organisation is desperate to hire. These days it may well involve assessing people's right brain skills more than before – imagination, empathy, seeing the big picture. Social psychopaths tend to be weak on tested empathy levels. Organisations are full of those who didn't get to do the tests.

- **Observation Point Eleven**

How do you get people to share your values? Find those who already do.

"You need to be able to do things such as forging new relationships rather than exacting transactions, tackling novel challenges instead of solving routine problems, and synthesising the big picture rather than analysing a single component".[7] These are fundamentally human attributes. They are not rewarded in all company functions. If you cannot bring people on a journey into an uncertain and chaotic future, every day, then you cannot expect people to follow you. Leadership requires followers. That is why CEOs were once called 'Chief Storytelling Officers' – CSOs? You also need to understand, as we note elsewhere, that people also have a tendency to follow psychopaths who create engaging stories. It's a complex world out there in corporate land.

When someone asks why marketing and communication support in security is needed they have failed to recognise the way and the how that security must be embedded in peoples hearts and minds. The cynical can counter by pointing out that a number of CEOs and their stories were huge yarns, and their supporting fabric equally fictitious:

"We do not tolerate abusive or disrespectful treatment. Ruthlessness, callousness, and arrogance don't belong here". This from Enron's 1998 Annual Report. [8]

Just as with security, leadership doesn't come with 100% guarantees, and stories don't have to be true to have interested listeners and believers. But in reducing risks, an assessment of human factors is as important as an appraisal of craft skills. When considering CSOs as leading management and senior executive candidates, performance in these kinds of areas is also crucial:

- Business acumen
- Perspective
- Relationship building
- Interpersonal style
- Judgement
- Values.

Against this additional background, it is the choices candidates have made, and make, in response to an array of challenges, that help to provide a clear picture of someone as a potential leading executive. People who find it difficult to do the following are revealing a lack of fulfilment for a senior role's scope and potential:

- Inability to form a collaborative team
- Reluctance or inability to share

- Disparate treatment of staff and colleagues
- Inability to accept blame.

People who are selected, or short-listed, for new CSO roles should be encouraged to take the same suitability tests a company expects its other mainstream managers to undergo. Yet we understand that in a number of cases there is a need to identify a specific additional set of qualities for the role, and there are bespoke tools to support this, which we have developed.

We have worked with psychologists, HR professionals, corporations, management teams, and respected security leaders to develop proprietary supports to aid the selection process for new security leaders and potentials. These supports complement other demonstrably effective selection criteria, and they represent an incremental level for filtering intangible craft skills. These can help reduce the surprise and costs that faced the financial services organisations we referred to earlier.

Reed Consulting,[9] a market leader in the provision of assessment services to private and public sector employers, estimates that employers waste significant sums on recruitment each year, and that in a survey, 21% of staff involved in recruiting had no formal training. When employers were asked if they had made the right decisions based on their assessment methods, 43% said they had not. When asked to estimate the cost of each incorrect hiring decision, 35% estimated it to be between $20,000 and $50,000, and that doesn't get anywhere near the most senior hiring levels. Importantly, these costs do not reflect the additional costs of damage done by unsuitable players for the time they were in place.

The introduction of new kinds of processes developed specifically by us for recruitment involving a high degree of security capability or management within the remit helps astute recruiters find better matches between company needs and the profiles of their candidates.

Formal succession planning within an organisation also produces multiple assessments from a variety of sources, and we say that the inclusion of specific security leader assessments makes the CSO selection process more rigorous and effective. We also believe the recruitment of successors should not be left to the incumbent CSO alone. If the current CSO is not integrated into the business it is more likely that resultant appointees will also be unable to reap the broader benefits of being embedded in the organisation and its culture.

The kinds of assessments we are talking about include both interviews and written tests designed to analyse further the kinds of human traits we have been talking about. The special knowledge required to handle this level of assessment usually requires outsourcing to professional assessors. Our teams also comprise highly skilled practitioners who have long-term and proven success in the management of major security challenges in successful national and international enterprises.

Before colleagues rush to confirm there could not be a better candidate for a role, check the recruitment criteria and process again. As companies push harder to attract and retain new high potential talent before their competitors do, with apparently fewer qualified candidates, wisdom comes from managing better those who claim that hesitation can only lead to loss.

A lack of specific, comparable, measurable knowledge about the overall capability of a security leader could significantly reduce the value they can bring to an organisation.

The Security Executive Council in Washington DC, US, produced its own version of a summary of the characteristics that best summarise the skills being demanded of a world-class CSO today, and for the coming generation.

We have added another list of characteristics:

Leader	Creative
Courageous	Innovative
Thought leader	Thrives on uncertainty
Considerate	Diplomatic
Fair but firm	Team player
Integrity	Intellectual rigour
Can do, will do	Strategic thinker
Personable	Insightful
High energy	Quick to focus

We welcome the inclusion of a significant element of human/personality traits. What is now needed is a structured approach to identifying and developing people who can meet and deliver the standards being recognised, but not yet being formalised, around the world.

In a number of ways, thinking about leadership and leadership styles has evolved to the point where, unsurprisingly, we see harmony with the factors that make a CEO, and any other respected quality leader, shine. That also means we see senior company managers in leadership roles as synonymous with the best CSOs, and vice versa. The times we live in call for a wider range of responses than some leaders seem able to muster.[10]

Limited leaders stay inside the organisational boxes their businesses designed for them. They "define businesses by their turf", perhaps leading their own team or division quite effectively, but then struggling when they come up against broader conflicts that arise. "More than ever we need leaders who can cross boundaries, who can help the parts work together by strengthening the whole". This sort of leader is a mediator. They do see the big picture. They do think systematically, and understand how the pieces of the puzzle fit together. "They are fully engaged in the thick of an issue, while remaining calm. They ask good questions, help sustain effective conversations, build bridges, and allow new ideas to emerge."

These eleven observation points need to be discussed, and perspectives reached about them, by all those who are charged with identifying, recruiting, and nurturing the next generation of security and secure leaders.

10. Further Perspectives on the Changing Role of Corporate Security

Have there been significant signs, gradual in their nature, that we have barely noticed but which have been changing our lives and the lives of those around us?

We are not in the soothsaying business, but we do believe that preparing for the unexpected today is a sound way of working towards a future over which better quality control can be achieved.

When people object and say it will take ten years to make changes, we have three responses:

- First, what we are talking about here represented major blocks and barriers ten years ago, and is now becoming standard practice in quality organisations.

- Second, the best place to effect a ten year change programme is from today.

- Third, if ten years ago you had said "What are we going to do about Al-Qaeda, and biometrics, and Weapons of Mass Destruction?" you would have been regarded as either strange or scarily prescient.

As an engineer once said, the best way to control the future is to invent it.

The winning organisation is going to master the challenges we have talked about so far, and will remain flexible enough to take on new challenges, those it knows about, those it thinks might occur, those it imagines and dreams and projects, and those that the world throws at it anyway.

This is a bridging point to some more of the changing perspectives that might reveal themselves to the enlightened observer. Let's take a closer look. The next generation of leaders will be expected to have the gift of a futurologist when confronted by life-threatening situations, criminal or terrorist actions, while many of their colleagues are free to parade the doubtful wisdom of what American workers call the 'Monday morning quarterback'. As we have said, we are not soothsayers, but we have allowed ourselves the indulgence of a little speculation under the wing of 'uncertainty management'. Here are some thoughts about scenarios for the near future.

The world just threw up a new surprise.

A mix of evolving events constantly affects us. We tend to record the seismic events. But some key changes have been barely perceptible outside specialist domains.In technology, the rate of advance and registration of new patents continues to accelerate at a rate that would have been unthinkable 100 years ago, even 50 or 25 years ago. Only the specialists are likely to know this.

Do you recall the remark of the head of the United States Patent Office around 1899 that "everything that needs to be invented probably has been invented" and that the office could be closed down? Why should you? The rate of mergers, acquisitions and consolidations over the past 10 years outstripped the rate of corporate activity in the 1970s and 1980s. New dangers arrive with newly acquired companies, especially if they come from less familiar parts of the world, from whatever your perspective might be – Russia, China, India, South East Asia, Iceland, Finland, Brasil, Ireland, Mexico, England, Spain. More change bringing less certainty.

Wealth has increased for many – poverty has also increased. Economic data shows that the gap between rich and poor seems to be growing wider. Does this not lead to increased instability? Hand in hand with wealth comes greed. Greed and corruption, those old established human characteristics. You are in the forefront of dealing with the consequences of greed and corruption. Greed and corruption show themselves dramatically, as we have catalugued, through the organized crime gangs that may control a region or a port, or a city, or even a country. Has there been a major change in our behaviour? Are we less ethical than our parents and grandparents?

Many of you may perceive a decline in ethical standards of behaviour. You, if you are security professionals, more than many within organisations, are expert observers of human behaviour. Has there been a change in ethical standards? Are we more or less ethical than 100 years ago, or even 50 years ago? If you detect a change for the worse, how has that affected your professional role? And what, if anything can you do about it?

There do seem to be many paradoxes playing themselves out here. On the one hand we seem to be becoming increasingly a global village. Yet on the other hand so much of our planet seems polarized by religious and cultural differences. Samuel P Huntington writes of the 'clash of civilizations' between Christendom and Islam. Others ponder on the resurgence of Islam from East to West. Some thinkers on Middle East politics ask the question, "Who won the Second Gulf War?" And they answer with one word, "Iran". What are the implications for security of a resurgent Iran determined to take what it sees as its rightful place as the regional power in the Middle East, and with nuclear power to boot? Your view depends considerably on your place and perspective of course. Regional politics inter-change in a flash with international politics.The only world superpower is resented. Some would say that is inevitable, just as the British at the height of their imperial power were resented, and so too Napoleon, and so too the Spanish, and no doubt Alexander the Great was not welcomed with open arms when he invaded Persia.

There seems to be a reduction, even a loss of community resilience. Is this loss corrosive? Don't weak communities lend themselves to higher rates of crime? What impact does that have on you? And what on earth can you do about it?

The rate of change makes it more difficult than ever to adjust and adapt solutions to new security threats. Why – because what worked last time may not work the next time. In fact there's a good chance it won't. Generals are often accused of fighting new battles based on their experience of their last war. Is that fair, even though it may be true? Is that a charge that could be levelled at you?

Take the illicit trafficking of radioactive and nuclear material. A leading thinker in the British defence establishment reminded his audience that technology alone cannot be the solution to better security. It is the mantra of almost every leading security professional, yet people still believe technology is more reliable then people. A corresponding change is also needed in how we think about and perceive problems and responses. And we need to rethink our experience because during a period of stability our greatest asset in problem solving is our experience. But in times of revolutionary change, this can be a dangerous hindrance.

Experience can be excess baggage. No one likes a smarty pants.

Because something worked last time does not mean it will work next time.

What about threats from organised crime and terrorism? Organised crime and the ever-present threat of terrorism are, perhaps, the most publicised dangers confronting us today, after state-led aggression. And they are increasing. However, for many enterprises, the stuff that makes Hollywood moguls get excited about box-office potential is well down the list of threats they really believe are critical to them. Things like liquidity, interest rates, exchange rates, transportation costs, employee health care schemes and so on get much more attention. Yet we still need to review what's going on.

You know already that any goods being traded on the black or grey markets are more than likely linked to organised crime, terrorist organisations, or both. Let's look at this from a psychological stance as well as a crime statistics stance. Some definitions may help to clarify this meaning. The criminal gang is in the 'illicit business' purely for the money and its own benefit. The terrorist is looking for political advantage, for influence. Although depending on the country, situation and culture, the roles can interchange. The old IRA in Northern Ireland and current Taliban Afghanistan are two good examples.

The thirst for power and control represents a menace of increasing proportion. Yet let us also acknowledge that this is seemingly a fundamental driver of human behaviour.

The amount of money being generated by illegal activity is staggering. Where does the money go? A conference of international tax planners in London talked about the problems of money laundering in offshore jurisdictions, especially in some small islands in the West Indies. However, the bulk of illegal money is generated in the wealthy and, some would say, profligate West. The money has to be laundered in large centres like London and New York. Perhaps those in the rich North are more part of the problem than part of the solution.

Today, the threat from counterfeit products grows. We have already illustrated some of the dimensions of this. But it's not a problem in the minds of the People. And it is not just the Intellectual Property argument that exercises lawyers. It is health, safety, and terrorism. The OECD commissioned a global study to obtain more accurate figures about levels of counterfeit activity. These kinds of figures will constantly be revised but are still likely to alarm for years to come, even if they are some way off capturing totally robust levels of accuracy. We are talking scale here. It's still BIG amounts of money:

- Way back in 2001 the European Union seized more than 95 million counterfeit articles, 10 times more than in 1998. By 2002–03 the number doubled. The trend goes relentlessly upwards.

- In the USA alone, the Federal Bureau of Investigation reckoned that the economic impact on legitimate businesses of losses due to counterfeiting is over $250 billion annually. The FBI describes counterfeiting as "the crime of the 21st century".

- Another example from the luxury goods industry: a raid on a Chinese Diaspora counterfeit watch gang in Manhattan found orders and pro-formas for business valued at $250,000 per day … and potentially about $50 million worth of business on the books for a year. And this was just one family.

- The government in Russia is said to forfeit about $1 billion per year in tax revenue due to counterfeit products.

- Distressing BBC World Television programmes show the extent of the fake pharmaceutical medicines problem in Africa, with products made in India and China.

- Spares for aircraft are being counterfeited. You don't want to spend too much time thinking about what happens when the turbo-fan replacements turn out to be duds as you are in the air.

Yet despite the vast amount of illegal funds generated, and the huge damage done to livelihoods, regional, global, not to mention local economies, the majority of consumers mistakenly see too much counterfeiting as a 'victimless' crime. There remains lot of work to be done here to change public attitudes and behaviour.

Focusing now on some specific industries and product categories, the picture should give us further cause for alarm:

- Take, for example, cigarettes. Whether you endorse or loathe the category, they are by value unquestionably the biggest product category for smugglers and counterfeiters. Some in the tobacco industry estimate that as much as 4% of world consumption could be counterfeit. That is about 200 billion cigarettes a year. Four times the size of the UK legal domestic market. No one is sure how big the total UK market is today.

- In the USA to take another example, 10% of the cigarette market is estimated to be illegal. That is about $76 billion in sales value – equivalent to half the GDP of Hungary, and about twice the GDP of Slovenia.

In the USA it has been reckoned that up to one third of all cigarettes in New York State could be illegal – whether grey or counterfeited. In the UK, which until fairly recently was one of the most orderly and profitable tobacco markets both for manufacturers and government, tax revenue and regulatory control of the market is sliding out of control. According to official statistics anywhere between 21% and 28% of the market is illegal. Loss in tax revenue to the government is estimated at about $5.4 billion per annum. Of course there is a double hit to the taxpayers as governments also increase expenditure on law enforcement, customs officers and police to fight the very problem that they have helped to create. In France, formerly a country with virtually no illegal cigarette sector, contraband is now growing slowly but steadily. All thanks to heavy tax increases and neighbours who have not followed suit.

Alcohol, though not on the scale of tobacco, has a large and lucrative contraband market. The EU estimates that its member states lose annually over €500 million in tax revenue from smuggled alcohol. In the UK, recent estimates of lost revenue were as high as €340 million so someone is either underestimating or overestimating the real numbers. In either case the level and scale of activity remains very high in anyone's terms.

Turning again to pharmaceutical products, the World Health Organization believes that between 5% and 7% of pharmaceutical products worldwide may be counterfeit, with particularly dangerous and alarming implications for public health. In 2002, the Food and Drug Administration in the United States launched 30 separate investigations into pharmaceutical counterfeiting, many of them popular brands. There is increasing concern among some of the major pharmaceutical manufacturers in Europe about the porosity of borders to the south east, east and north east of the recently enlarged European Union. Global estimates of losses to the industry are around $12 billion per annum.

Let's restate the reasons for growth in the illegal trade. The financial incentive is of staggering proportions. Here's a starter. Some $120,000 is all that is required in China to manufacture sufficient cigarettes for a 40 foot container. That is 8.5 million cigarettes, or 425,000 packs of 20. Shipping and 'facilitation', in other words, bribery costs, are already included in that number.In the UK the recommended retail of price of cigarettes in the premium sector is over $8 at today's rate of exchange.

If these fake cigarettes can be sold at, say, $6 for a pack of 20, the net profit can be as high as $2,430,000 with little risk.The next logical question is, where can these cigarettes be sold profitably? Well, wealthy Europe is surrounded to the south, east and north east by a ring of much poorer countries.There is sufficient financial incentive to get profitable but illegal goods across porous borders and not very long distances.

The growth of counterfeited products is alarming. So too is the range of products being faked. Not only cigarettes – alcohol, ladies cosmetics, baby food, coffee and tea, car components, olive oil, shampoo, batteries, clothes, shoes, garbage bags, pasta, golf clubs, motorcycles, and luxury leather goods, but also more life critical products.

This is just one more link to the much broader world of illegal and challenging activity.

The police who in the past seemed reluctant to draw direct links between terrorist funding and contraband are a little more open now and say that there were links between 9/11 and gangs involved in contraband activity. Defining the problem and relationship between organised crime and terrorism is not easy for governments. But the point of terrorism – maximum impact on so called legitimate economic or civilian targets in Europe, the USA and the Middle East – makes closer cooperation between organised crime and terror organisations more not less likely.

This raises some simple but vital questions to international companies:

- Are you doing enough?
- Is the company doing all it can to protect its employees abroad, and to protect its brands?
- Can governments do more?

- Should you be working more closely with governments to influence their policies that affect corporate securities?

- What kind of formal, policy or advisory associations exist, or need to be created to communicate the needs of organisations and enterprises better and to hear from government about their concerns?

As the nature of the security problem becomes more complicated and sophisticated so it will demand better and better responses from government. Effective solutions require deeper thought and analysis. This is an area where business should work even more closely with government to get over the problem of being reactive or defensive. Business people can take advantage of the trust that the public can have in their national security forces that they may not have to the same extent in the business community, to bring resources, knowledge, and expertise to the aid of the government.

If it isn't troubling enough that criminals are all around us on the ground, they also seem to be all around us in cyberspace too. There is a new frontier into which extremists and criminals have moved: the sophisticated use of the Internet and cyberspace. These attacks are launched from a safe distance to neutralise control of essential economic infrastructures using pure IT resources. Computers are as vulnerable and sensitive as people.

Financial services, power supply, transport, emergency services, food and health are all reliant on computer based equipment which in turn is increasingly susceptible to hacker attack, viruses and worms, as well as bandwidth clogging and digital traffic jams.

The digital traffic jam caused by the MS Blast worm was often cited as another contributing reason for the dysfunctional US power stations that were unable to balance the load on the 14 April 2003 and caused the largest power-cut in history. The cascading failure led to the collapse of electric power in the entire North East of the USA and affected other cities like New York, Detroit, and Toronto. The UK, Sweden and Denmark as well as Italy and Switzerland had power outages near the same time.

Fundamentalist hacking and phishing activity is rising and has been getting more sophisticated over the past five years. Criminal organisations from Kashmir, Pakistan, Morocco, Turkey, Chechnya, Saudi Arabia, Kuwait, Indonesia and Malaysia are collaborating both with each other and fringe anti global organisations based in the West in order to target international and domestic online assets.

Large and small-scale businesses, government computer networks as well as home computer owners have all been targeted by organized crime syndicates and radical hacking organisations. The identity theft, the financial fraud and business interruption damage exceeds tens of billions of dollars in each category.

Identity theft, phishing scams targeting over 20 major banks in the world and credit card fraud are all rising. They provide cover for licit and illicit organised crime and extremist activists. As much as 25% of organised criminal syndicate activity is perfectly legal, and it is licit because it has a safe façade behind which nefarious activities can be carried out without challenge.

From spam to malware proliferation, the use of home computer zombies is growing. Every single computer on the planet can be recruited for malevolent crime and extremist activities either as an end target or a go-between for launching Distributed Denial of Service attacks followed by extortion or ransom demands. A number of companies have already paid up. 11.5 million zombies are used for illegal file sharing and mail relays. And the cost of digital crime is in excess of $250 billion per year.

This is a modern, almost post-modern phenomenon. Perhaps these types of security threat have already hit your own company, or companies you have invested in. Maybe it is something that some of us are not comfortable discussing in a wider circle. Because the security of corporate information is so important, as are the consequences of the latest technological innovation, it is vital that someone, or a team, is positioned at the forefront of new ideas in the respective organisations to manage and thwart the growing problem.

These problems are both generated outside and inside enterprises. Let's look again at corruption inside the firm, and implications for security professionals. There was a time when your corporate colleagues, Executive VP Marketing, Executive VP Business Development, Executive VP Finance, Executive VP Sales, and even the CEO had more modest ambitions to just run the business profitably, provide the shareholders with consistent dividends, and take home good bonuses at the end of each year.

Since the frenzy of M & A activity, all that has changed. Many corporate executives have now made great advances thanks to mergers and acquisitions. Their interests may be much more short term than before. And their interests are much more for personal gain because of the large amounts of money that can be made. This is the point at which we come right up against personal greed in the higher echelons of management.

Because the M&A market is becoming more and more competitive as companies search for new targets to acquire, special schemes, perhaps even special favours, are still being created to gain advantage or to win contracts. A company is expected to be protected from attack by a number of different sources. And yet it may be difficult for some of the appointed protectors to 'break into' the very top end of the senior management circle before it is too late.

Perhaps one can often only deal indirectly with the potential problem of senior management who in their efforts to maximise profits, or strike the big deal or acquisition may also be creating liabilities for the company, the shareholders and the employees.

There are other dimensions which may complicate matters further:

- When a company is about to embark on a major relationship with, or intends to buy, another company, is the CSO involved in the due diligence?

- Do other senior management members come to the CSO before the fact or after the fact? Perhaps there are awkward conflicts of interest at the top that should be brought out, but for various reasons are suppressed.

- Are people aware that there is more to due diligence than the balance sheet, P & L, Return on Investment, and other important ratios?

- Organised crime is growing increasingly adept at putting its place-men in the higher echelons of corporations.

- A company can be made extremely vulnerable if it does not know what kind of foreign networks it is dealing with, and whether it is unwittingly grafting onto its healthy body a malignancy with organised crime or terrorist connections.

Checks by due diligence audit firms or lawyers alone will often not find out that information so easily. It is important that people with relevant skills, knowledge, and experience are brought in at the beginning, and are working at the very highest level within the company. It is a question of knowing. The security resource should be a key first based source of this 'knowing'.

So what should a better future look like?

- It is clear that information and the technology to use and move it will accelerate.

- It is clear also that governments will seek to try to draw more and more power under their control to protect citizens – whether efficiently or not is another matter.

- There will not be a reduction in terrorist activity in the foreseeable future, but it is not the key threat for many enterprises.

- Certain foreign nationals and their property, in particular Americans, and some others will be seen as more legitimate terrorist targets than others.

- Businesses will come under increasing pressure as energy and other utility prices climb, and margins are squeezed.

- Security operations will continue to be expected to do more with less.

- The criminal mind will continue to be ever more resourceful dealing in businesses that bring the greatest returns for the least risk.

How do you deal with this? We say again, a change of mentality is needed. Just like, NATO, for example, an organisation many would think had no conceivable role today, is thinking more deeply than ever before about the nature of its response to the emerging security threats to its members, and engaging with the private sector on these challenges.

Though governments have the elected authority and mandate, private enterprise often has a sharper motivation, is closer to the problems, and has the variety of networks to provide solutions. Sometimes this may mean collaborating with the authorities, sometimes the problem can be solved by acting unilaterally. Use resources and insights to help bureaucracies to be sharper and more focused and more relevant. They are often a lumbering machine. It is important to find ways to be more nimble and responsive.

This means broadening and deepening thought processes used to understand and solve problems. One way is to increase the building of links with the best think-tanks and universities, to have access to the best brains and original thinkers on and around issues that are crucial, not only in a forensic sense, but also in technology, social and psychological sciences, risk analysis, defence establishments, and the best business schools.

Engaging with the media should be seen as productive, not something to be shied away from. They are crucial to an improved understanding on both sides. They have a wealth of information but often not a deep understanding of issues. But they understand how to communicate. And they have access and an audience.

Initiating and encouraging regular cross-functional exchange in corporations at the highest level can expand understanding and co-operation. This may well also bring a new dimension to colleagues by raising the bar of knowledge and intellectual challenge, thus forcing them to admit that they had never looked at a particular problem or issue quite like that before until they had the insight and opportunity to look.

Legislation and regulation are key drivers of the emerging awareness and significance of disaster recovery and business continuity in a wider range of businesses. Disaster recovery traditionally focused on ways to recover from IT failures, but now continuity has extended to embrace enterprise risk management, and operational risk management as well as data security. Some are urging to call it 'corporate resilience' and turf battles for ownership continue as specialist suppliers extend their offers and consolidate services. This is another area where a well executed continuity plan can attract lower insurance bills, but also give a competitive advantage in areas like corporate social responsibility. The vice-chairman of the Institute of Operational Risk, said that business continuity and operational risk are two sides of the same coin – "There has to be greater integration. That is the way forward."

"There is a world of difference between appearing to comply with a given standard and creating and implementing a strategy that both works and is practical," said the CTO of Data Genetics International. But too many continuity plans are too complex to adhere to in the face of a real crisis.

In this chapter we haven't even begun to look at other threats, viruses, natural disasters from earthquakes to tsunamis to global warming challenges and resource availability and management. There are a lot of significant threats we haven't catalogued here, but each one is subject to the need to practice fresh collaborative thinking to enhance our ability to handle whatever comes our way. We continue to visit and revisit core issues to look at them through different eyes, to take different perspectives, to see how they look when they are presented to us at different times and in different formats and shapes. Our responses are shaped by context, and we must be careful to understand the nature of our observances.

Be an integrator. But as Einstein said, "Things should be made as simple as possible, but not any simpler."[2]

11. Standards in Security: Do You Measure Up?

Influence as a core competency is the heart of the measurably effective CSO. Metrics are a tool used to facilitate influence, to demonstrate, argue, support, and convince.[1]

What measures or metrics can be applied to help demonstrate to management and other interested parties that security is bringing value to an organisation?

As the Security Executive Council points out, "Security metrics are not about numbers: they are about performance". Interestingly, established and widely applied metrics and measures have been rare to uncover until relatively recent times, which suggests that either security was deemed unworthy of 'metrication', or its practitioners were considered to be non-core. With the risk environment now significantly different from what it was even five years ago, the need for compliance and the demands for the demonstration of contribution are beginning to grow. To move from being a cost of doing business to a net contributor needs to be supported with convincing demonstrations of effectiveness.

Like a professional pilot, the commanding security leader needs to have the key cockpit panel of information and checks that must be constantly monitored, and is most suited to the current environment and circumstances, type of business and key security threats and opportunities. Anything monitored will need to make sense to others who also have to review the data. Information can then be introduced into their own metrics reporting for management, whether that is through a finance department, legal, audit, direct to the Board, or any other function.

Measures need to be sensitive enough to contribute to an understanding of the delivery of core business objectives. They need to be fast enough to collect and appraise to enable a speedy and wise response for corrections or adjustments to be made in a meaningful time and cost frame.

Such measures might include

- an analysis of security costs as a percentage of total company revenue
- due diligence examinations
- background checks
- physical security and premises protection
- attributed contribution to incremental share growth, volume increases, and productivity
- governance and compliance conformity
- corporate reputation and responsibility.

Along with honed leadership skills, this is the only way a security leader will be able to convince a number of metrics driven managers that the corporate security operation represents a value centre in the organisation's overall operation.

The influence and value of the security function will be directly proportionate to its measurable impact on the organisation's ability to manage its business and its risks. That's how many others will want to judge it. In these terms, security adds value when its activities enable the business to be more profitable (productive), and add value to reputation and governance.

The right metrics will allow you to determine

- What, where, how and why risk is occurring, or might occur
- Service quality and customer satisfaction
- Deliverables of new and existing programmes
- How much money/ and resources should be spent on or assigned to security
- Which system components should be targeted first
- How exposure is defined, and whether it is being reduced.

Where the anticipation of risk is a basic expectation of managers and shareholders today, measures embedded within the organisation's structure that can help eliminate such things as plausible denial, in the US especially, will support the overall measures in place to monitor compliance.

The right measures will also help manage risk across all its primary manifestations — strategic risk, organisational risk, financial risk, and operational risk. Since security leaders have to work with other experts in these areas, influence as a core competence is a major requirement in the new generation of leaders, and metrics are a useful way to facilitate influence for all those who need to argue, support, convince, or be demonstrated to. Once the 'protective' security measures are working, relevant metrics for added value can be introduced.

Having captured all that, it is worth repeating that the best metrics are those that have been edited down to critical useful levels. Tracking 137 metrics a month is not going to be the answer. Defining the ten to fifteen critical performance indicators is what counts, in the same way we noted for the airline pilot.

Specific   Metrics are specific and target the area you are measuring

Measurable   Collect data that is accurate and complete

Attainable   Have metrics that are easy to understand

Relevant   Don't measure things that are not important

Timely   Timely data and current for responsive action

For a collection of types of metrics and performance indicators appropriate to security, the Security Executive Council in Washington DC, USA, has produced a valuable body of work on developments in this area, and for non-members Google provides a multiplicity of metrics that can be considered according to organisational circumstances. Included in those is the ability to be predictive. A readiness for new and emerging risks is a key ability, but it needs to be aligned with credibility in an organisation, influence, and relevance to the or

Take comfort from Shirley Payne's SANS Institute Guide – "Because developing and maintaining a security metrics programme could take considerable effort and divert resources away from other security activities, it is critical that the goal(s) and objectives of the programme be well defined and agreed upon up front. Although there is no hard and fast rule about it, a single goal that clearly states the end toward which all measurement and metrics gathering efforts should be directed is a good approach. A goal statement might be, for example – 'Provide metrics that clearly and simply communicate how efficiently and effectively our company is balancing security risks and preventive measures, so that investments in our security programme can be appropriately sized and targeted to meet our overall security objectives".

General Electric, one of only six triple-A rated US industrial companies, and one of the world's most admired, invested over $15 billion in intellectual foundation and filed 2560 patents in one year alone. In an operation which values hard and soft values equally, the CEO himself says "Leadership in security and crisis management is about consistency, planning and exercising... it is about developing a process". Security in GE touches all these points to ensure it is an enabler of growth for the company:

- protect technology
- enable globalisation
- excellence in performance innovative solutions
- visionary leaders
- focus on customers.

In addition, what keeps Frank Taylor, GE's global head of security, and his team busy are the range of challenges which arise daily in the face of a global presence. These include handling natural disasters from tsunamis to swine flu, terrorism and crime, or both, repeated attacks on security, especially IT, but also on other assets, together with how to develop ways to work in and with emerging markets, both on the ground and in cyberspace. In terms of aligning security with the business, GE has a very harmonised fit. "When the process is inherently capable...issues are caused by inconsistency – but when the only way to improve is through a new process, you need to create 6-Sigma capability."

With 6-Sigma, there is an almost religious focus on measuring the process output and measuring the data, discovering quantitative relationships between the output and the in-process variables, and developing and implementing a control plan. In this context what makes a great security leader is defined as "the ability to develop insightful strategies that support the company's goals and objectives which lead to surprising results". Data is used to drive decisions from an outside-in perspective.

Over at another major player, Starbucks has the challenge of protecting not only its 140,000 employees and 13,000 stores in 40 countries, but in caring for the 45 million customers a week it serves, and getting the 228 million pounds of roasted coffee safely in their hands. Their world-class security system has delivered gross contributions to the company of significant scale. Their approach is also guided by an interesting cultural context which essentially asks "What's the right thing to do in a culture where we do the right thing?" This in turn is worked into an operating mantra which encapsulates these essential elements – protect people, secure assets, and contribute margin. It is an intelligence-led approach to security in complete synchronisation with the company's overall strategy.

This all translates into an enviable customer benefit –"There's a great sense of security when you go there", psychologist Joyce Brothers says. "It has given people a safe place to socialise." [2]

One CSO wanted to prove his value-added credentials and those of his department. He was a traditional corporate cop type with few of the characteristics we have been citing and applauding here, but he did at least realise there were advantages to being able to show he was adding to the bottom line. Having applied his brains to the challenge he found the solution.

All members of his security management organisation world-wide were required at the end of every report to add a line indicating how much money had been saved as a result of their actions. His response to every draft report he sent on up the line was to amplify security's value with the simple addition of a zero after each stated sum.

This is not what we mean by value from security.

12. Designing a Profitable Multi-Functional Security Organisation

Here we look further at ways to engage people and how to make sure the best areas of opportunity for an environment can be designed and implemented, in the context of a background of continual change and challenges.

There are one or two first-class sources of detailed technical information on building a world-class corporate security function that we fully endorse. Here we return to our over-arching themes of harnessing human resources and establishing networked coalitions that can help pull this together:

- How can you tap into all that useful brainpower in your organisation, wherever it operates, to create a sustainable core security function?

- How do you overcome boundaries to openness?

The ability to act requires resources and investment, which in turn requires making a compelling business case to key decision makers. Here we look further at ways to engage people and how to identify the best areas of opportunity for an environment, in the context of a background of continual change and challenges.

'Security Design' will increasingly become a core function serving both the drivers of protection and the drivers of value creation. This is a concept and strategy that embraces risk management and mitigation, as well as incremental value creation. Whatever the size and style of the organisation, there are certain principles that will apply to them, and of course implementation variants that will play out differently in each host environment.

Let's return to some of the rich learning from John Roberts[1] in his seminal work *The Modern Firm*. Some of his statements may appear to be obvious, but are borne out of a lifetime of observation and analysis, presented in a highly palatable fashion. For him, strategy and organisation are critical, and there needs to be a close fit "between strategy and organisation and between these and the technologies, legal and competitive environment." Like us, he is at pains to point out that changing core elements is often not easy or swift, but that change sometimes has to happen, and it can do so positively.

The point is made that an organisation is a collection of People and organisational features that can be sorted out into Architecture, Routines and Culture (leading to the taxonomy PARC). There are the hard and soft features like governance and networks and decision authority. In this collective environment, the challenge is to design a security service that will maximise performance. It is clear that to do this, security cannot be the responsibility of the CSO alone, but needs to be the responsibility of the CEO and other managers throughout the organisation.

Roberts' analysis suggests that "over the long haul, honest managers who pursue the maximisation of firm value are likely acting to create the most possible value for shareholders."

To achieve success in implementing a security strategy that will profit the organisation, it will be necessary to test its robustness through what we shall call a 'complementarity test'. Essentially this means that two selected variables, let's say, protection and value creation, become complements when doing more of one of them increases the returns to doing more of the other. In contrast, substitutes occur if doing more of one of them reduces the attractiveness of doing more of the other. Roberts points out by way of example that direct monitoring of employees' behaviour and the use of performance-based incentive pay may be substitutes. Without being able to demonstrate the principles of complementarity in a new security strategy, it is unlikely that those in a profit responsible role to vote it through to implementation will be ticking the 'Yes' box.

Adopting and championing changes that appear to be positive and worthwhile needs leadership skills of a high order. First among these is a need to get the organisation to the point where there is a strategic recognition of the need to adopt a new model. Getting to 'Yes' then must embrace the skill of vision to see the potential of taking up the new route. Getting to this stage and then making the idea permeate the organisation needs strong communication skills, and the empathy skills we have noted earlier. There is a need to explain the new path, what it looks like, how to go along it, and what one might expect to see along the way and at the first and second of a continuing line of destinations. This process itself takes courage, and that includes the strength to continue along the path and not to retrace steps or abandon the route at the first gate or fence. "Changing established patterns of behaviour means learning how to operate in new ways and how to communicate with new people about different things. This can be a slow and costly process."

The inevitable human dimension recurs. Resistance to change that in some real or perceived way endangers the position, power and pay of those in the organisation can also dilute and degrade the strategy. Take an example from another sphere of influence. "The immense majority of intellectually eminent men may disbelieve in Christian religion, but they conceal the fact in public, because they are afraid of losing their incomes," an observation made by Bertrand Russell.

Fortunately, we are only dealing with security here... change will always be a threat to some people in an organisation, however much it is presented as an opportunity.

It is worth combining the thoughts of John Roberts with the organisational historian and analyst Simon Schaefer. "...the prospect of change creates opportunities to influence the new distribution of resources, power and rewards, and members of the firm will have every incentive to attempt to ensure that they and their allies do well."

"A crisis is a good thing."

"Sony will turn the 'perfect storm' of problems in its battery and PlayStation divisions to its advantage", said Sir Howard Stringer, worldwide chairman and chief executive, who hoped to use recent crises to accelerate changes he began.. "The crises created opportunities which I think we've taken advantage of", Sir Howard told the *Financial Times*. ..."Under the shadow of the crisis we're able to get things accomplished that might (otherwise) have taken a little longer", he said."[3]

Change may be easier in a crisis scenario. The gains to resisting or reshaping changes could depend on the organisation's very survival, so that changes that would not be worthwhile to attempt in good times will be implemented when survival is in danger. This requires cool-headed leadership. Once again we find ourselves describing a world where, whatever the security competences of the CSO might be, the world of change comes through the equally necessary set of leadership qualities we have explained earlier in terms of CSO or security leader characteristics.

Getting sign-off to the security strategy gives you permission to proceed to the next critical stage, which means executing the strategy in a cost-effective fashion, while simultaneously creating as much value as possible. This means being able to motivate the organisation so that they consciously elect to behave in ways that support their belief in a value-adding security strategy.

This is always difficult where people's personal point of view about how they wish to behave may not help maximise the total value generated for the organisation, for example, about how much time they are prepared to invest, and what risks they are prepared to take. BP found that encouraging employees to take responsibility and exercise initiatives worked best when values of caring, trust, openness, teamwork and cooperation were espoused.

Treating security managers as asset managers could lead to them being encouraged further to rely on peer organisation colleagues for support. In BP's case, the whole organisation was structured around peer organisations to facilitate mutual assistance among member assets and to promote the sharing of best practice. The concept of peer challenge was also introduced so asset managers' collective expertise and knowledge could be applied to setting future strategy and targets. Levels of mutual trust in this highly successful organisation increased. Then it all went wrong. Something else took priority place for behaviour and attention – profitable growth *at all cost,* an agenda set by the CEO, with an ultimately personal costly outcome. The operating culture appeared to deny security's ability to balance goals and behaviour, growth and compliance.

It is necessary also to exploit all opportunities in the current organisation and at the same time explore and develop new opportunities. Since these are different kinds of tasks, needing different kinds of skills and approaches, any activities pursued along these lines will deliver reduced success when an organisation does not reflect a similar shift in how people and resources are deployed. Get the right team to deliver maximum performance on the current security strategy – that's exploitation. Get the right team to look for new value-creating opportunities – that's exploration. This is a creative action that needs analytical skills as well as skills of persuasion. It comes back to the mantra of Secure Leadership. Some managers will be excellent at crafting and designing the execution elements of the strategy, but be weaker at controlling networks and cultural elements in the organisation. Others may be more adept at helping people determine what they are going to believe, value, and adopt. Leadership plays a key role in harmonising these strengths and efforts, and in giving specific meanings to values, not merely mouthing intangible concepts. This is a reiteration of the security leader's ability, like the CEO, to tell meaningful 'stories' rooted in real examples of behaviour.

Get used to the idea that security and creativity must become mutually supportive partners to create new value and to keep it.

Those who do the same things in the same ways as everybody else are neither better than rivals nor guaranteeing the improving value. In fact, parity security may increase the chances of exposing an organisation to threats and attacks. Security strategy needs to be about balancing the proven and the tested with new and different things that work. It is a skill of blending and combining.

Seeing new patterns and connections is a key part of a security leader's skills.

It is a distinctive trait, and needs to be turned into distinctive security activities in and for the organisation. Think of the security role as being the Chief of Perspectives, and how that weaves the player into the heart and fabric of an enterprise.

In this regard, much more work can be done to understand how information is shared in organisations, and what surprising behaviour can emerge from detailed analysis.[4] "Suppose that some of the people in your organisation are deliberating about some factual question; suppose too that each member has some information that bears on the answer to that question. Will members disclose what they know?"

"For each person, the answer may well depend on the individual benefits and the individual costs of disclosure. Suppose that you disclose what you know about a problem that your company is facing. If you do, it is possible that you will receive only a fraction of the benefits that come from an improved decision by the organisation. And if each organisation member thinks this way, the organisation will receive only a fraction of the information."

"When this is true, participants in deliberation face a standard collective action problem in which each person, following his or her rational self-interest, will tell the organisation less than it needs to know. There is a lesson here about how to improve deliberation. If organisation members are rewarded for telling the truth or for moving the organisation in a direction that turns out to be the right one, then deliberation is likely to benefit from the knowledge of many more minds, which has major implications for institutions, corporate boards, work places, and governments."

The discussion goes on to other situations that force us to reconsider accepted norms. For instance, a team player is often thought to be someone who does not upset the organisation's general consensus, "But it would be possible, and a lot better, to understand team players as those who increase the likelihood that the team will be right – if necessary, by disrupting the conventional wisdom." The highest performing companies often have contentious boards that regard dissent as an obligation.[5] A key question is how to alter people's incentives in such a way as to increase the likelihood of positive dissent or disclosure.

It may be difficult to make this happen if you are a new player in an organisation, or it may be easier – that depends on the organisation's preferred operating style. Change is sometimes only tolerated when it is delivered through familiar faces and mouths, where in other circumstances the new fresh voice is fully welcomed. There may be some HR-funded material or people who can help the new voices integrate into the culture, but we would counsel an additional contribution from an external security professional who is in a position to mentor or coach a new CSO or security leader in a new role.

Such a person can usually bring valuable learning, because they have performed a similar role successfully in another operation and can bring valuable experience to helping the newcomer embed in their new role. In a number of cases, the same person will have special knowledge or background experience that can also help the one being coached in specific technical areas. Last but not least, there may be an empathy in shared experiences and knowledge, for which the human resource department alone cannot provide the specialist skills and knowledge internally. This is proving to be a valuable adjunct to established training or induction programmes that organisations provide for their people.

Independent board members typically provide oversight and monitoring of a company, while managers run operations. But when a crisis occurs, such directors are increasingly adopting a more hands-on role. Stronger governance standards reinforce the trend. "Your wealth is at stake, and your reputation is at stake", says Charles Elson, head of the Weinberg Centre for Corporate Governance at the University of Delaware. Done properly, this is another role of management counselling, especially where management is overwhelmed by the crisis at hand. This works best when the same directors are dedicated to both their fiduciary duties and the company's future. Gaps in a board's collective experience can be filled in this way, and those with previous experience of crises can provide valuable experience and insights.

Strategic Leadership Agenda

The security drive team envisions, energises, enables and focuses efforts to achieve goals that will result in obtaining the "preferred future."

Let's turn finally to planning now, and look at how a fresh perspective in an, 'alpha' global organisation could yield constructive and surprising results to support the design and creation of a security management strategy that will be totally integrated with the objectives and challenges of the host organisation.

We said we wouldn't give comprehensive checklists in this book, but for all the process hungry, here's a half way house, a topic list of what should be considered in the next plan, and some rationales for the form and structure. As we said at the beginning, we recommend a number of sources for extended technical details in these areas.

If you don't need this, or don't like plans like this, go to the Secure Advantage Summary chapter and beyond, which is predicated on all that has gone before, and takes up much less space.

Security Strategic Design and Planning
(Due Diligence and Exercises to consider)
Contents

1. General

The best corporate security operations recognise that, building on foundations of success, they must be properly aligned and integrated with their host organisation's strategy and values in supporting and shaping the future of the operation.

A best practice corporate security operation must:

- Be business focused, aligned and integrated.
- Provide the momentum and motivation to ensure the business recognises its value.

The more successful the corporate security function (csf) becomes at aligning itself with the business and integrating itself into it, the greater the function will be regarded by the business – truly a case where success breeds success.

To achieve this level of success, action is required in many areas. The process starts by examining the existing security infrastructure and progresses by defining an enhanced methodology, involving other business disciplines, for the development of a number of business-critical security objectives that will deliver a required optimum.

2. Executive Summary

- A strategic corporate security plan will be completely aligned with the organisation's overall strategy and builds on the foundations of the existing corporate security function, especially where that is already strong. Implementation of the plan will further enhance the function and ensure that it continues to be properly integrated into the business at every level within the organisation.

- Both internal and external situations will have been examined, taking into account the existing security risks/threats facing the organisation and attempting to project how these may develop in the future.

- Security managers will be developed into cross-functional team players, becoming indistinguishable, in terms of business expertise and knowledge, from the managers of any other function.

- Enhanced recruitment measures, supported by HR, will ensure that the best possible people are recruited into the security function at all levels and that they are properly trained and developed to the highest technical functional and business standards.

- The plan ensures that all members of the csf and their line managers will have access to a 'Security Knowledge Base'. This will provide the latest security information and techniques that can be delivered, supported by the latest technology.

- Enhanced methodology, with the security function leading on investigations and enforcement actions, will better enable to organisation to counter threats.

- Crisis management, another key area in which the csf can enable the business to thrive, is properly addressed to ensure appropriate multi-functional training is delivered wherever it is required.

- The organisation's corporate responsibility will be enhanced by the implementation of the plan. This is particularly evident in the areas of employee protection, investigations, anti-fraud measures, information/IT security relating to standards of business conduct, and activities on Human Rights.

The processes that will best deliver the plan are summarised in the following sections and provide 'traction' for the implementation of an entire strategy. These processes are themselves integrated as there are functional and managerial relationships between all elements. In line with a business integrated approach, concurrent implementation of many elements is necessary.

Of course, this plan serves an 'alpha' organisation, and variations will need to be generated for the specific needs and positions of the range of organisations looking to achieve higher levels of value from security. In this regard, the templates are included as agenda suggestions. In the following sections we have moved away from the discursive style of the major part of the rest of the book to keep the narrative succinct. However, most of the material we have included has been driven by experiences, many of which we have cited in earlier chapters, that reflect the need for the careful consideration of, and response to, these specific areas, to design a comprehensive and actionable security operation.

3. Statements and Objectives

Vision Statement
To enable and support leadership of the ******* industry or service by providing outstanding, value-adding corporate security

Mission Statement
To deliver excellence in the management of security, ensuring that people and business are protected, so enabling greater growth, profitability and enhanced reputation.

Key Objectives

The key objectives of the organisation's strategic security plan are to:

- Ensure that people and business interests are protected, focusing on business critical areas, including crisis management and business continuity.

- Develop first class business security managers to become an indisputable part of the organisation's winning team.

- Attain full alignment and integration into the business at all levels so that the csf is regarded as a core business service, not a cost of doing business.

- Facilitate the enhancement of the organisation's reputation as a truly responsible company.

4. Internal Situation Analysis

In turn, the organisation needs to be able to demonstrate that it has an excellent security strategy, plan, and policies that are fully supported by the Board. An excellent security infrastructure must exist throughout the organisation, preferably a benchmarked one. Databases that contain best practices, procedures and sound advice on most aspects of 'hands-on' security management will need to be constructed. These are widely used by security managers and appreciated by others.

When compared to other competing organisations, the security function of *********** should be as well integrated into the business as it is in most other leading enterprises.

The csf should be represented at Board level in every operating unit by a director responsible for security who is appointed by the Board. Some are appointed because they want the role and some by default. It is clear that where directors recognise the value of the function and encourage its development, the best results are achieved. With the successful development of the right people leading to senior security managers taking up positions in top teams, the director responsible for security may well be the senior security manager.

It is essential the director responsible for security has a genuine buy-in to the value of the security function and fully understands the role of representing security at Board level. 'Buy-in' and empathy are crucial requirements. In many big organisations there has been a perceived need to subordinate the security function to another key function i.e. if the CSO reports to the Chief Legal Officer, senior security managers in markets and divisions would often report to the senior legal manager. This might be neat and tidy but can also result in a greater risk than other options of losing buy-in and empathy. It should be remembered that the only reason CSOs and other senior security managers may report to someone heading another function is because CSOs are not generally in the "C-Suites" or on the Board, and other senior security managers are rarely in their market's or division's top teams. Other than the need for top team representation, there is no more logic in security reporting to HR, Legal, Finance, Corporate Affairs etc than there would be in those functions themselves reporting to Security.

Within an operating unit, the day-to-day management of security should be carried out by either a Security Manager (a full time security professional) or a 'Manager of Security' (a 'double-hatted' manager and not a security professional.) These security managers report to a Director responsible for security. Security managers need to understand the requirement for business integrated security and ensure the continuing integrating of the security function into the business must remain a primary objective of the overall organisation's csf. The degree of security integration frequently determines the level of credibility and status that security managers enjoy.

Integration is achieved when the security managers demonstrate a high level of professionalism and deliver a high quality service. These factors, combined with a strong personality and with good influencing skills, enable other business managers to recognise the value of the csf more easily. In 'high risk' markets or businesses, security is already considered vital to the businesses' success and survival.

5. External Analysis and Threat / Risk Analysis / Matrices

An organisation may face a wide spectrum of concurrent threats. The threat spectrum is constantly evolving and has the capability to deliver multiple impacts simultaneously at multiple levels – on individuals, communities within the organisation, or on the core business itself.

A key foundation of security is the ability of managers to have a profound understanding of the threat environment historically, currently and very importantly predicatively – making 'over the horizon' assessments. Without this ability, security will remain reactive rather than preventative, and not able to deliver to its full potential as an added value creator.

The csf must fulfil four key requirements to address the threats that face the organisation properly. These are:

- Timely and accurate threat assessment
- Pro-active threat prevention
- Multi-layered and robust threat effect reduction
- Rapid and successfully focused crisis management.

Threat Assessment

Threat assessment must be a continuous process where security managers accurately evaluate the spectrum of threats by:

- Identifying and defining the nature of threats.
- Assessing the frequency and/or probability of these occurring.
- Determining the likely impact so appropriate defences can be designed.

The organisation's csf should have a threat assessment process where all threats are categorised within these eight broad classifications:

- Criminal threats to persons
- Criminal threats to assets
- Political and societal threats

- Military threats
- Technology threats
- Terrorist threats
- Illicit trade threats (where relevant)
- Natural threats/disasters.

The world is changing and the threats are changing with it. The organisation will also be changing and the csf must be ready to adapt and adopt to address the threats. In the future, it is likely that:

- The world will be even more unpredictable with threats becoming increasingly cross-border and international.
- The global developed community will remain a community of sovereign nation states with the 'have not' nations remaining the majority.
- The globalised economy will retain strengths and capabilities, and greater threats to diminish it or destabilise it will be likely.
- National disorder, with accompanying violence, will not be impossible.
- Organised crime and terrorism, like from extreme protest movements, will still be able to exploit weaknesses in international public sector cooperation.
- Increasing dependence on cyberspace with rapid technology changes will continue to occur in both an anticipated and unanticipated manner e.g. IT and robotised manufacture. This will be accompanied by increasing exploitation through organised crime and major terrorist organisations, exacerbating existing risks and presenting new ones.
- Greater regulation of business, nationally and internationally will result in more specific regulatory frameworks that will demand demonstrable and appropriate security controls aligned with risk.

To meet the challenges that the above will bring, the response from the security community overall is likely to include the following:

- Common acceptance of "Corporate Security is to Companies what National Security is to Nations" and security professionals being given greater resources to deliver solutions that reflect this insight.
- The csf's of multi-nationals will be universally business integrated and aligned, and having to meet far greater expectations.
- Security will become a profit multiplier, a reputation enhancer and a projector of corporate social responsibility i.e. a more recognised and looked for factor in shareholder value.
- Most CSOs and heads of security promoted from within business, and many CSOs on Management Boards or "C-Suites" will be in place for their merit as cross-functional team players as opposed to simply their worth as functional experts.
- Company planning processes without security involvement from the outset will be

unthinkable. Outset security will become more generic.

- More opportunities for leadership roles in corporate security will arise for recruits from other business functions, supported by technical experts.

- Crisis management skills will be a requirement for all middle and senior managers in other functions.

- There will be less and less separation between corporate and IT security.

- The nationality of CSOs and other senior security executives will be more varied in multi-nationals.

- There will be greater cooperation with, and support for, small and medium sized enterprises (SMEs)

- Security will be a bigger component part of major MBA programmes.

- Outsourcing – scope will depend on excellence measured against higher demand and expectations
    - the outsourcing of security management at lower levels might be more prevalent.
    - outsourced provision might be managed by in-house resource

- The organisation will have representative and authoritative bodies for engaging with the public sector – nationally and internationally.

- Public/Private Partnership Dimensions:
    - Business security will be reflected in national intelligence collection plans.
    - Public/Private sector will be in more effective regional (e.g. EC) partnerships with business representation , including the security industry, embedded into the assessment and decision making processes (including associated vetting) – nationally and internationally.
    - Private sector involvement in PPP will see greater participation from Universities, Churches, and NGOs etc.
    - There will be more joint training between public and private sectors.
    - Security secondments between public and private sectors will occur routinely, and be of mutual benefit.

6. Business Alignment and the Cross-Functional Team Players

To address the threats to the organisation's security and for the csf and its members to progress within the business, it is vital that correct business alignment is achieved and all security managers develop into capable cross-functional team players.

Given an understanding of the mission, vision, and strategy shown in an organisation's strategy, a key component of the business security requirements should be a security risk and threat analysis. This is a continuous process to determine likely security environments and threats, how these could impact on the business, and how the impact should be mitigated. We have given many examples of such scenarios in the preceding chapters.

A formal security risk and threat analysis should be presented to the Board for endorsement prior to the start of the process that results in the production of the organisations overall annual plans. An action plan should then be agreed and performance objectives/key result areas should be linked to its delivery. A suitable template, developed to ensure a standardised approach, is required for this task.

Most senior security managers should be able to address business risk. Audit and security should cooperate on training and awareness programmes. While the disciplines remain distinct, there are crossovers that would benefit from greater coordination.

Although the csf will never generate profit directly in the same way as the Sales Operation in many organisations, security can be a profit multiplier, a reputational enhancer and a business enabler. It is therefore vital that the csf remains ready to seize every opportunity to perform and be identified as a critical contributor to business, once its core function of maximising asset protection is achieved. Security's potential to contribute to reputation and goodwill in non-profit organisations is also to be highly encouraged.

To facilitate alignment between a Director responsible for security and a security manager, a security management element should be included within a Director's role profile, or remit.

The senior security manager should be included in all 'Top Team' meetings to help:

- Develop a greater understanding of the business in general.
- Gain a better appreciation of other functions and how security impacts on them.
- Encourage better networking with other Top Team members who then gain a greater understanding of the csf.
- Provide a basis for excellent working relationships with other business partners internally and externally.
- Ensure a much easier integration of the csf into the business.
- Establish productive personal relationships with individual Directors/senior managers and discuss issues with them individually.
- Provide an excellent service for all functions.

To be properly integrated and aligned with the business of the organisation it is vital that the csf is:

- Identified across the business as being a core service, vital to business operations , and regarded as totally integrated within every aspect of the business and adding value in all that it does.
- Able to demonstrate value for money in an organisation committed to reducing operational costs by working smartly, and using shared services or leveraging purchasing power when buying goods and services, where these make sense.
- Continually identifying talent and has a structure which provides career opportunities comparable to managers in other functions.

In order to address the dynamics of change, the csf must look ahead to be properly positioned to:

- Recruit from other business functions and ensure there is adequate security development available for these recruits.

- Ensure corporate and IT security become a unified function.

- Identify a selection of security recruits and greater development of local security managers to promote a more multinational selection of function members, where relevant

- Develop and achieve gender balance

By improving standards within the security function through the ongoing training and development of security managers, it is possible that within the next five to ten years there could be more Chief Security Officers in the "C-Suites" or on the Management Board of the organisation.

Recruitment

One of the keys to achieving success in all aspects of the organisation's csf is also to ensure that security managers are of the highest quality. Ideally, they should be indistinguishable in terms of business expertise from other managers, and deliver a service of equally high standards. This starts with the recruitment process, and we have given considerable space to discussing the qualities required for the emerging generation of security managers in the preceding chapters.

By recruiting the best quality people for the security function, the process of creating a winning team becomes easier as they will:

- Represent the csf well and deliver a more professional service.

- Increase their knowledge of the business and create better integration opportunities, having the intellect and leadership abilities to do so.

- Have greater influence on their colleagues and be well accepted by other functions.

- Improve training levels both within and outside the function.

- Enjoy greater career opportunities and generate a higher quality of recruit in the future.

- Contribute more to the business and become of greater value to the organisation generally.

When necessary, external recruitment agencies should be used to assist in the identification of potential candidates, who are then short listed for interview. These processes require close monitoring but if an appropriate agency is selected, the results can benefit the organisation in a number of ways. We have considerable expertise in this area of operations, and we are happy to share our knowledge with organisations wishing to benefit from this experience.

The recruitment of second career managers can add value to the organisation, where cultural fit can be achieved. While in some cases there may be reduced expectations in terms of further career progression, organisation experience can be gained rapidly and good service can be delivered over a number of years. Even in these scenarios the selection process should remain parallel to that used for other candidates.

As part of the recruitment process, talent spotting by existing members of the organisation's security function to identify suitable candidates should be carried out. Consideration should also be given to advertising a security vacancy internally and approaching known individuals in the organisation directly. Candidates with IT Security experience must also be targeted.

Role profiles should be produced or revised prior to the recruitment process starting. These should include the core competencies for the delivery of a business integrated security service. Role profiles should not only reflect the skills required, and accurately identify the role, but should also show clarity in the level of business integration expected.

A very rigorous selection process is necessary for all security appointments.

Selection will usually be by means of a properly constituted assessment service, facilitated by HR, ensuring that the individual characteristics required are the equal of equivalent manager roles and individuals. The assessment service interview panel should consist of senior security and other business managers. This reinforces to the rest of the business that security managers are selected in the same way as others. Inclusion of managers from other disciplines, thus demonstrating a multi-functional approach, helps to ensure that only the most suitably qualified candidate is selected for a specific operating culture and environment. A suitable format for an assessment service is required. Our own dedicated security search and selection practice does precisely this – www.secureleadership.com

The interview process should be as standardised as possible so that all candidates get asked a similar selection of questions.

For those from demonstrably security based backgrounds, not less than 50% of the questions should be based on security technical competencies and should be prepared beforehand, together with bullet point answers. In this way the non-security members of the Panel understand what answers are expected and the answers given by the candidates can be more easily measures.

The security technical competencies should be reviewed and linked directly to the role profile.

Induction Training

On joining, the training and induction requirements of all new appointees should be determined. These should be noted on a formal training and qualification record that is properly maintained during the manager's career. It may be the case that sessions of coaching and/or mentoring over a period will be utilised to support the newcomer's ability to deliver the desired security service quickly. In addition, a training and development programme should be developed for every member of the wider organisation's csf. This should include specific and mandatory training requirements for all security managers.

Providing high quality functional and management training for security managers will improve their overall standards. Security managers should follow a formal training programme that should include the following:

- Induction processes in the organisation that will be run by the CSO, assisted by other security managers. A suitable format for an induction course is required.

- An induction in the organisation's business should include an attachment to a core function, like Core Services, Marketing or Finance, as this would also enable the security manager to understand the business better. Again, a suitable format is required.

Security Industry Regulation

The private security industry is regulated in many parts of the world, usually by means of a licensing authority that manages the licensing of individual security practitioners and companies. In most cases, regulation also aims to raise the standards of professionalism and skills within the security industry and to promote best practice.

Despite this, members of the organisation's security team may not be part of the national security Industry and as in-house security managers are not usually required to undergo a licensing procedure. There is merit in at least some managers undertaking the procedure in the interests of demonstrating professionalism and as a means of relating to other managers in the security industry.

Organisation Specific Functional Training

All security managers and identified individuals and teams from other core functions require substantial organisation-orientated training in crisis management/emergency planning/ and business continuity. Carrying out this training is a very large commitment and requires significant resource.

Certain security managers, who have the appropriate background, should undergo training in other skill applications such as investigations and enforcement, anti-illicit trade, counterfeit, and other specialisms.

To address these training requirements, a security training manager should be appointed, internally or outsourced but who must be a very experienced security manager with detailed knowledge of the organisation and crisis management plans/procedures. This manager should:

- Train throughout the organisation.

- Scope, plan, produce and where appropriate, deliver all training material/courses.

- Produce and run crisis management and business continuity exercises and the testing of plans.

Functional Career Development

In-service training and development should continue along security specific and multi-functional lines, with participation in courses designed to increase knowledge in the fields of Marketing, Finance, IT, Corporate Affairs and other core business areas. A wide variety of business training programmes should be made available. At Burrill Green we offer such support services or are able to recommend other best in class service providers globally.

The direction in career development depends upon how the business believes security within the organisation will change or develop within the next few years.

Managers of functions other than security should be encouraged, when they have the aptitude and where training and mentoring opportunities exist, to take positions in the csf.

To deliver a professional integrated business security service requires a skill set which should be supported internally and externally through public sector intelligence and security/law enforcement skills. Those assigned to the function without this additional support will require supplementary training if they are to meet technical expectations, or the provision of such experts as part of the delivery team.

As a bridge to broader integration, security managers would benefit from participating in seminars and training opportunities provided by other functions. This education process benefits business security integration while providing a window into understanding functional realities and ways security may integrate and align better.

The careers of all security managers should be determined through the career development process which is used for all business managers.

The csf should ensure that there is a coordinated approach to career development systems that incorporates the organisation's general processes and appraises every security manager to identify those with potential, and for development and succession roles. Feedback, including recommendations from this process, should be provided to the relevant operating units for the benefit of the individual and the csf as a whole.

Not everyone can be a leader all of the time and some security managers may never get the opportunity to progress beyond a certain stage. Given the acknowledged limitations for some security managers to progress either within the csf or in another function, consideration should be given to rewarding good work and encouraging them towards development in specialist skills that would continue to benefit themselves and the organisation in support roles.

Dual Role Appointments

A Manager of Security, versus a CSO, is a means of providing security cover in non high-risk operating organisations. This is a dual role position where a manager from another function is given responsibility for some security duties, (typically guarding, alarms and fences) in addition to his/her main role. This has tended to reinforce the old perceptions of security being about only locks, bolts, bars and guards, and will take time to change.

The Shared Service Approach

An alternative approach is to provide a full time security professional as a Security Manager who could be shared by two or more operating units. While this delivers a greater level of security expertise, the following challenges are sometimes encountered:

- Balancing of priorities between stakeholders and from this, the balancing of time/ resource allocations.

- Management time and effort is required in ensuring that the Directors responsible for security are aware of the need to balance the requirements with the needs of the other operating units.

- The Directors responsible for security must communicate well with each other and should hold regular review meetings, in the presence of the functional manager, to ensure that the system is working effectively for all parties.

- To integrate fully and to play an active role in more than one operating unit, the security manager must devote a lot of time to building relationships.

- The security manager requires strong communications / interpersonal skills in order to operate successfully. Building relations and sustaining these is a requirement.

- It is necessary to understand different cultures and working practices.

- As the security manager cannot be at one location 100% of the time, there remains the requirement for trusted, competent security representatives on the ground in order to implement security strategy/recommendations and conduct the day to day management of guard forces etc.

- The number of issues and projects, normally of a diverse nature, that are ongoing at any one time requires a very flexible approach.

- Developing good local contacts internally and externally is essential.

- Understanding the evolving local business needs that are related to plans and developments takes time and good contacts. Without these it would be hard to be truly business integrated.

- Strong functional support and knowledge of the individual operating units is essential. Attempting to manage all stakeholders, with their varying needs and personalities, can be frustrating and almost impossible without this support and knowledge.

Some operating units are now placed in clusters that are managed by the leading market or division/unit in a cluster. Consideration should be given to managing the security function by means of:

- Shared service agreements between operating units, divisions and clusters.

- Appointing security managers to functional positions, e.g. Operations Security Manager.

Some multinational organisations, particularly in extractive sectors, combine the roles of Security and Environmental Health and Safety (EHS.) Future development and training should not exclude the possibility of further cooperation in this area.

7. Organisation Security Databases

Security Core Knowledge Management

The ability to source, collate, analyse and disseminate quality information to stakeholders in a timely manner is a key challenge for the csf. In an age when media information is delivered directly to mobile phones and PDAs this means that alarming breaking news – correct, partially correct or incorrect – is rapidly available to organisation staff. The csf needs to be at the leading edge of information dissemination to provide timely security and business intelligence within the organisation. Failure to do so will mean that security is increasingly reacting and responding to the need to correct and clarify other externally sourced information inputs to staff rather than being a leader in providing timely and credible information.

There are three main areas of knowledge that must be managed:

- External information sources
- (media, government agencies, NGOs, service providers)
- Internal information sources (organisation information, excluding security)
- Company security information.

The csf must develop systems ensuring that security information is available in a one-stop shop IT-based resource that offers the opportunity to share key information elements with internal (audit, AIT, Top Teams) and possibly external partners.

Where appropriate, a global travel tracking solution should be introduced so that, as far as is possible, all organisation international travellers can be traced at any given time.

The csf should move towards the active delivery of targeted information to internal stakeholders rather than expecting stakeholders to come and trawl databases for any information that may or may not be available for them. With this in mind, security information should be supplied via a Security Knowledge Base.

Leveraging Existing and New Technologies

The increasing use of wireless hand held devices to access information services is an opportunity for the csf to deliver more efficient access to and dissemination of time-critical security information (crisis management plans, threat warnings etc).

8. Anti-Counterfeit / Anti-Illicit Trade (where relevant).

Counterfeit can represent a major financial impact on many trading organisations. Primacy for the investigation and enforcement against crime, including illicit trade, is a core csf competency.

The csf should lead and support on all local end-market investigations and enforcement actions.

The csf should lead on those engagement programmes which enhance the capability of the organisation and external stakeholders to investigate and enforce against counterfeit traders. Stakeholders within this category could include Customs, Police, other Law and Regulatory Enforcement bodies, Judiciary, Justice Ministries, Intelligence Agencies, Diplomatic Missions, external service providers, other trade and industry bodies.

To deliver in this area, high calibre individuals with excellent investigation, intelligence, business liaison, negotiation and networking skills are needed.

9. Crisis Management

The delivery of effective crisis management (including emergency planning, disaster recovery and business continuity) training and response, is a business critical contribution to the business.

The csf should identify and prioritise key people to undergo crisis management education and training. These should include the following:

- Board Directors and senior managers from other functions
- Security managers and Directors responsible for security.
- Appropriate unit and operating company/division staff.
- Top Teams.

Training should be based on priorities identified following formal threat assessments that the organisation as a whole and end-markets should complete on a yearly basis and be carried out within the framework of a formal and scheduled training program.

Crisis management training modules, each of which can be modified to satisfy local requirements, situations, and management organisations, can be formulated as:

- Kidnap and ransom
- Malicious product contamination
- Other extortion incidents
- Major fraud
- War, civil and military unrest
- Terrorism
- Industrial unrest
- Operating unit closure
- Disaster recovery/business continuity (including IT aspects)
- Hacking and aggressive virus infection
- Supply chain security (Security managers /Directors responsible for Security).

Response

The csf should further develop the concept of cross-boundary working so that security managers can be tasked across the organisation's boundaries in time of crisis responsibility.

10. Leverage Of Functional Objectives/Activities In Support Of Organisation Corporate Responsibility

The csf can provide support within a number of areas. By leveraging the size of the organisation and the reputation of the organisation security function, various financial advantages can also be gained.

Leverage of security objectives in support of organisation corporate responsibility is all pervasive and can impact on all members of the organisation, particularly Top Teams in the following areas:

- Corporate governance, where it is necessary for the csf to be aware of the requirements of the organisation's corporate governance model and to leverage this in order to present the csf role as business-integrated.

- Corporate social responsibility – particularly within activities on Human Rights.

- Protection of staff, an area in which security has always taken a prominent role, particularly in ensuring staff travelling to or living in high risk areas are properly briefed prior to travelling and appropriate protection is provided on arrival.

- Security of the working environment, where the csf provides the guarding, and physical/electronic security measures have long been a showcase for the function. (This provides further opportunities for leverage as these services are usually outsourced.)

- Crisis management, disaster recovery and business continuity all require the security function to play a large part in the planning and execution of the measures required to address these issues. (If your organisation does not require this involvement: re-think)

- Privacy, sometimes relating to procedures required for privacy of the person (searches), personal space (workplace, car, home etc), and information about individuals (Data Protection), information owned by individuals (Personal Use) is well known to the csf.

- Education of staff and the provision of awareness to business managers, on the subject of what is permitted by law, should already be being provided by security managers. Advice should also be provided on the monitoring of employees and reassurance/involvement of HR, Legal and Corporate Affairs in defining and operating processes like the investigation of staff. We have commented on the pitfalls of this around global operations in the previous chapters.

- Information security, in particular insider information, mentioned in Standards of Business Conduct.

- Security Risk Mitigation, where the security risks are reduced to appropriate levels is a core requirement of good corporate governance.

- Investigation and enforcement, usually protection against fraud, theft, misuse or abuse is a security core technical competence skill.

- Reassurance and benchmarking, activities regularly carried out by the security function, provides a comparison between Company 'A' and the good practice observed in other similar companies.

- Due diligence for mergers, acquisitions, outsourcing projects and with current business partners.

11. Functional Outreach

It is important that the security product is seen and appreciated by all target audiences.

The security product can be packaged as follows:

- Advice on security issues, protection and business enabling
- Risk assessment (including the intelligence process)
- Benchmarking against others
- Security education, training and awareness
- Crisis management training and operations
- Emergency contacts
- Investigations
- Liaison / external contacts / influence
- Monitoring and enforcement
- Policy and best practice, experience and expertise
- Protection of people, assets and hence the bottom line
- Reassurance
- Risk mitigation
- Reputation management
- Security leadership, both within the organisation and also in the corporate world
- A corporate conscience in the protection of reputation.

The target audiences are:

Other functional managers (including IT, Audit etc.)

- Top Teams / influencers
- Line managers
- Employees and contractors
- Business partners, suppliers and contractors
- External authorities
- The Public Sector.

The organisation will benefit from a Security Appreciation Course that should be available for everyone, and especially:

- Potential General Managers
- Finance Directors
- Directors responsible for security
- Management trainees (to attend at least part of the course, or a bespoke course)

- Auditors
- Insurance managers (internal and external).

Security should also work closely with key business partners, suppliers and contractors to raise their understanding, standards, and the quality of their products. Exerting leadership in standards will ensure mutual benefits and protection of the interests of both parties. It will also assist the development of Preferred Suppliers and Partners allowing the possibility of reduced costs over a wider market.

Operating units also benefit by providing specialised security training for business partners, particularly in high risk markets.

When units profile their business with a local interactive website, business security should feature and there is considerable value in spreading the practice widely. Publicising who delivers the service, what is delivered, its intended contribution to the business, plus topical input on relevant events helps embed the function in the minds of employees.

All security training programmes and courses should be included on the HR master list of training opportunities and programmes. These should also be collated and made available for reference via any best practice data bases.

The sensible rotation of Directors with responsibility for security would provide security managers with exposure to a wider range of business functions and also provide more Directors with the experience of representing the security function at Board level. This should assist greater integration. (There may be a danger that a Director with little enthusiasm for the security function is appointed, thus presenting the security manager with additional challenges to the primary purpose). The rotation of Directors responsible for security should be addressed by means of a succession plan

It should be routine that basic security questions are raised with Audit as part of their compliance reviews. A centrally agreed matrix of measurement should be applied.

With corporate responsibility and reputation management playing increasingly important roles, the carrying out of proper due diligence checks by the csf on potential business partners is a critical issue.

The importance of pre-employment background checks for those being recruited or moved into high risk positions within an organisation is also vital for the business. Working in conjunction with HR and other functions, security can provide significant input to these processes.

Reports produced by the Audit Teams are identical in format and style so that all concerned know what to expect, recognise the format and can readily identify recommendations requiring implementation. Likewise, to reflect security's business integration, there should be an agreed reporting process, readily understandable to other business managers.

An organisation security 'Brand Manual' should be developed that includes key messages, logos, tag lines and how the function should be promoted and represented.

12. International Networking – Private and Public Sectors

Vertical, diagonal and horizontal integration within the organisation should be essential to providing a business integrated service that adds value to the corporate effort. Security managers must also be integrated externally in order to provide comprehensive advice to organisation decision makers and to meet the objectives and spirit of the business' Security Policy Statement. Barriers to communication are simply unacceptable.

In order to integrate externally, security managers must cultivate contacts within both the public and private sectors. Within the private sector, excellent liaison with the security professionals of other companies is essential to keep informed on risks/threats and mitigation measures.

Networking should be included as a core activity function that is measurable and evaluated for annual performance reviews.

The most useful areas for networking and contact opportunities include:

- Law enforcement agencies at both local and national level.
- Government and commercial intelligence and security entities.
- Diplomatic missions, particularly embassies/High Commissions.
- Security related government sponsored gatherings for the private sector present a good forum in which to network with both private and public sector representatives.
- Membership of and involvement in activities of professional security organisations (such as the ASIS International, Information Security Forum, International Security Management Association, International Association of Chiefs of Police; or local equivalents) and industry bodies are encouraged.
- Liaison with international organisations such as the EU, UN, WCO, Interpol, NATO etc.
- Chambers of Commerce and Confederations of Industry.

As a development from the increased level of networking, the security function should work towards increased levels of Public/Private Partnership dimensions, particularly:

- Public/Private sector being in more effective partnerships with Business, including the security industry, embedded into the assessment and decision making processes and incorporating procedures such as vetting, both nationally and internationally.
- Business security requirements reflected in national intelligence collection plans.
- More joint security between public and private sector, leading to security secondments between public and private sectors taking place. Outsourcing of Central Threats and Risk Assessment and Dissemination.
- Targeting other organisations that could help the business link with potential PPP partnerships, such as NGOs etc.
- Promoting security as a component part of major MBA programmes.

13. Cost / Benefit / Metrics

A form of cost/benefit metric analysis should be a critical and routine process. In addition to demonstrating value for money every year, it also identifies all the areas to which the csf contributes to the organisation. When linked to positive results it makes the task of the function easier by justifying expenditure when aligning with the business.

Exercise Summary

If the due diligence and these exercises reflect most of the points we have covered, clearly adjusted for scale and geography, then the organisation will be well down the path of creating a plan for the delivery of excellent integrated business security that will both protect and add value to the enterprise. This has been a generalised trip through the world of strategic corporate security development, so of course there is no one ultra version, or painting-by-numbers design to follow – each organisation has different needs and different preferences. We are here to support the process of development and dissemination, particularly in understanding and managing the human factors and dimensions in creating and managing a successful strategy and policies.

This has been our most prescriptive chapter, and if it appears dry, it can best be tempered by revisiting earlier parts of the book, where the experiences and lessons in real time, and with real organisations and scenarios, have formed the basis for this rational distillation of recommendations and suggestions.

Where you feel we might have missed out areas or opportunities, we would of course be delighted to hear about them so the experience and practices can be made available again to others who are seeking to enjoy higher levels of value from security. You can do this through our website at www.burrillgreen.com

---

Get used to the idea that security and creativity must become mutually supportive partners to create new value and to keep it.

---

13. Security as a Brand

In the same way that brands permeate every area and aspect of the companies that own and nurture them, security is displaying family likenesses to brands and brand values. Brands are all about trust, and security is no different. Brands can also be said to be the sum total of the information people carry around in their heads about them, and the experiences they have had with them. Brands do not exist in a merely physical form. Neither does security.

Let's face it, crime and criminality aren't going away any time soon, so the management of a secure environment in which to conduct business is a significant challenge even for a company whose activities are confined to one country, region, or even town.

These days, the best security no longer looks just like a fence or fortress. Security requires both a protective element and an enabling element, integrated with the overall business. It is becoming more pervasive than it ever was. Consequently, it is less to do with simple checks and procedures administered by a detached department, and more about an attitude and behaviour that affects everybody, and is everybody's responsibility.

Security should no longer be wholly owned by one department. A car is not 'owned' by one section of a car manufacturing facility. Neither is a chocolate bar, or a computer.

If security is to be seamlessly pervasive, and everyone is to be responsible for it, how can we be sure its presence and role have been clearly communicated and instilled in everyone, and that people will confirm through feedback their consistent understanding of the security role in their organisation?

You may have many views on what security's role might be. Here is a way of regarding it that can make a tangible difference to its role, effectiveness, and acceptance.

- Would your security operation match the same levels of knowledge and interest as the products, brands and services you create, in a survey about what your people know about the organisation?
- Treat security as a brand, as a branded service, and look after it in the same way.

Brands are only as good as the people who trust them. It's the same with businesses, with leaders, and with nations. It's the same with security.

This perspective can help people feel more comfortable with security, and their responsibilities towards it, in an organisation, community, or other networked environment.

"If we are to move beyond self-interest, communities must be united by trust"[1]

We see one of security management's primary roles is as a trust enabler.

Trust does not reside in integrated circuits or fibre-optic cables. Although it involves an exchange of information, trust is not reducible to information. Since communities depend on trust, and trust is determined by culture, it follows that trusted security management will look and feel different in different companies with different cultures.

The most effective companies are those based on communities of shared ethical values. But the absence of clearly stated ethics also produces companies that can be very successful for a time. These have tended to have names like Enron, Tyco, Worldcom, Parmalat, and BCCI. They can also bear the names of individuals like Bernard Madoff and Sir Allen Stanford.

If people who have to work together in an enterprise trust one another because they are all operating to a common set of ethical norms, with good products and services, a business should enjoy sustained success. Not only that, this approach actually reduces the cost of doing business, with no loss of quality, standards, or reputation.

Security as an enabler of trust should be regarded increasingly as an important lubricant in an organisation. Managed properly, proven ways of addressing security management opportunities can increase organisational efficiency, enabling people to produce more goods, or indeed more of whatever values are held in high esteem. Last but not least, in environments with increasing regulatory demands, security management can also help reduce transaction costs.

Security's strategic role as a trust enabler supports entire organisations. Inappropriate reductions in security or trust lead to the appearance of more intrusive, costly rule-making and regulation.

In this scenario, it is less easy to put security in the same box as all other things that are considered merely as cost-centres.

How can security be marketed around the organisation, and with key external audiences? Here is a brief look at ways to do this.

If there is no talk about marketing and communications with regard to security, there is a dangerous gap in the way security is seen and treated in an organisation. Sharing among risk-taking organisations – everyone, is crucial.

Audiences should become participants in and with, as opposed to passive recipients of, security marketing and communication programmes. It is essential to earn the trust of all the audiences involved and demonstrate that security can listen and is open to feedback – it should not be a one way process. People need to learn over time what is going on, and by learning through their individualised experience, security can become an embedded strategic element of the organisational culture and its behaviour, a desired response.

Technology plays its part in communication, but its role is subordinate to credible content. There needs to be a communications manifesto aligned to the business and where relevant, brands and the specific security brand variant that fits a particular organisation best.

Every brand has a story to tell. Using other brand professionals to help can make the security story, or case, more interesting. People are saturated with messages these days and it is important to find fresh ways to capture their imagination. It is important to encourage taking liberally (legally of course) from other industries like music and film and using their techniques to create marketing campaigns that people can enjoy and believe in, and expect others to mould as they get involved and re-tell the stories to others.[2]

99.9% of company audiences probably have other jobs to do than security, as they see it, so they are looking for simplifications to make all the other things come together in manageable ways. Strategies and programmes need to be created and delivered with this understanding. Security then becomes an acceptable part of everyone's remit, not just the responsibility of a department with that name on it. It is vital, if humbling, to realise that most people don't really care about the business of security, and certainly not its messages, unless they are given convincing and motivating reasons to believe and try. Creativity will also help stop the security service from being regarded as a commodity, and the secret is that everyone can be creative.

Lucid Incorporated discovered through research that for all people, regardless of their jobs and whether they are thought of as ingenious by others – *to create* is as basic a need as food, water, and sleep. It just needs to be managed properly, which can still be a challenge in corporations that do not nurture creativity throughout the enterprise. Once again, the leading security players will be masters of sharing in seeing positive results emerge from this kind of creative involvement, activity and approach.

> ### *We see one of security management's primary roles as a trust enabler.*

14. Secure Advantage Summary

By now we are clearly stating that the most profitable corporate security strategy emerges from the establishment of networked coalitions. For starters, these should include senior management, cross functional organisations, and preferred partners – the target audiences should extend throughout the organisation and its whole customer base

Why this approach?

Simply because there is a need to offer added value services from security to the board and to shareholders for at least these four reasons:

- To support the need to be competitive in the marketplace
- To satisfy stakeholder agendas
- To justify investment in security
- To demonstrate an improved return on investment (ROI).

Added value can only come from strong foundations.

What factors from this base will lead to a successful, integrated business security culture? We have noted that:

- Seeing the need to perceive security as a business enabler is a critical first step.
- Seeing that it is a core function is step two.
- Seeing security as a value enhancer is step three.

Taking these steps means being able to say that security now sits at the heart of an organisation's continuity and crisis management capability. It also necessitates the security leader being regarded as a senior cross-functional leadership team member. It also demands that security is intelligence influenced. Security can be a driver as well as a follower – or its potential remains underutilised.

Security should be a major contributor to thought leadership for an enterprise.

Delivering this model needs outstanding people and practices, supported by bespoke products and services. This means ensuring maximum efficiency and performance for the company in its most exposed areas.

'Best in Class' will look different for different enterprises, different products and services, and different markets and geography. However, the essential value chain designed and executed for security management in the business will deliver benchmarked excellence in all these areas. Here is an example of a prototypical Security Service Value Chain:

Security's Service Value Chain

For each link in the value chain of the organisation, there needs to be a deep analysis of what responsibilities and actions, people and capabilities exist, and the impact of their behaviour on the company's overall security and values.

In the example above, for instance, the top left box lists 'suspects'. This says there is a need to know as much as possible about who is out in the world who might be interested in the organisation, for good or bad, where they are, why they might behave in a certain way, when, and what the organisation is prepared to do about it.

The next box along to the right raises the subject of prospects for the organisation and how it might treat them differently from suspects. These may be customers, or they may also be suppliers or potential partners and employees. In each box there will be people inside the organisation who work with functions, machinery, or people, who will enable the deepening and refining of the model so the organisation can build robust ways to protect the chain and its links.

There will be a need to define tipping points and triggers for solutions at each place in this chain, or any extended chain that is developed. The dynamics for measuring success will include the ability to get more from existing resources, and a demonstration of a tangible contribution to the bottom line and the organisation's overall value set. Working with a small organisation to get these foundations right will eventually reinforce the ability to safeguard the strengths of the company, support regulation, compliance, and risk, and continue to develop an added value security skills base.

At the end of the journey of conducting due diligence on the operation, it should be possible to say, "The main justification for any changes is to reduce risk to the company's future economic development. This will be achieved by encouraging orderly diversification from security's established traditional protective role, to enabling roles giving rise to further valuable opportunities."[1]

> ***Security should be a major contributor to thought leadership for an enterprise.***

15. Security Principles and Key Points

This book has been driven by a set of principles that fundamentally underline our approach and attitude to the contemporary business of delivering Value from Security. Whether you read the book from cover to cover or cut straight to here, you will now find the summary of our principles and the key points the book is making, derived from all the practical experience and examples we have set out in the preceding chapters.

- Security can be a ubiquitous source of incremental value.
- Security's role is to protect assets and nurture values.
- An intelligence-influenced organisation has a Secure Advantage.
- Value from Security is everybody's responsibility.
- Successful security is embedded in the organisation's culture.
- Outset security must be an integral part of any planning process.
- Security due diligence is a must.
- Security is a Brand. Its key values are trust and transparency.
- Security's role and contribution must be measured.
- Security must make sense.

Key Points

We now repeat the key statements from the earlier chapters that appeared in bold, and in summary boxes at the ends of some chapters. These indicate the elements of our case for achieving greater Value from Security in practice, and pragmatically :

14. *Security can and should be business driven and not compliance driven.*

15. *Security is a significant area of unrealised incremental value today.*

16. *Added value comes to secure sharers.*

17. *Professional corporate security management should play a core role in forging the links between the way a company or organisation does its business, the quality and the depth of its relationships with the community, and its ability to operate in a safe and sustainable way.*

18. *Modern security is the business of rationalising paradoxes, pragmatically.*

19. *Ask yourself, next time you are faced with a challenge "What kind of response do we need, what kind of organisation is needed?" as opposed to "How are we going to preserve our organisation against this threat, or change?"*

20. *Security is no longer a side dish.*

21. *Corporate security is to corporations what national security is to nation-states.*

22. *The function of security management is to create and maintain a secure condition in which people are safe, the business will flourish, the organisation's reputation will be enhanced, and opportunities for improvements, like with governance, will be identified and acted upon.*

23. *Security and shareholder value are entwined in the most successful companies.*

24. *Security can enhance the benefits of transparency.*

25. *Security is about the successful understanding and management of motivations.*

26. *By understanding motivations it is possible to design better security management capabilities.*

27. *How can you simplify, and contribute to, your organisation's ability to manage challenges that affect its core values?*

28. *The new security leader needs to be a master of building bridges, an engineer of trust.*

29. *Corporate security and national security should become networked security.*

30. *Security takes on the task of trying to make sense of the conditional.*

31. *More convergence enhances trust through transparency, which is, or should be, a core business and organisational value*

32. *The poor management of risk has a negative impact on the achievement of business objectives and ultimately on shareholder value*

33. *Security must be embedded in the operations of the company and form part of its culture.*

34. *Security is part of an organisation's DNA.*

35. *Security's potential role as a driver of transparency may come as a shock to some people, but we regard its contribution here as one of enhancing the long-term protection of company assets and values.*

36. *Security is not an option. It is a right.*

37. *Get used to the idea that security and creativity must become mutually supportive partners to create new value and to keep it.*

38. *We see one of security management's primary roles is as a trust enabler.*

39. *Security should be a major contributor to thought leadership for an enterprise.*

If you have got this far – congratulations.

Notes, References and Acknowledgements

Notes and References

We are indebted to many of the ideas and findings that further shaped or supported our thinking, some of which are contained in these sources:

Forewords

1. Francis Fukuyama, "The End of History and the Last Man", Free Press, 1992

Preface

1. Brian Tracy Quotations (Google)
2. John Gribbin, "The Universe: A Biography", Penguin Books
3. Centre for Digital Strategies, Tuck School of Business at Dartmouth, USA, 2006, and the Institute for Information Infrastructure Protection
4. MIT, "Enterprise Security Perception and the 'House of Security'", 2006 c/o Cisco: CSO Custom Publishing - Cisco Public Information, "Measuring and Evaluating an Effective Security Culture" White Paper
5. Cisco CIO at the time of writing

Book Structure

1. EM Forster, "A Passage to India", 1910

Introduction

1. "The Council on Competitiveness", USA, 2006
2. "Cutter IT Journal", May 2005

Chapter 1. Security in Business – Cost or Contributor?

1. Security definition, Oxford English Dictionary
2. Antoine van Agtmael ,"The Emerging Markets Century", Simon & Schuster UK Ltd. 2007, Chapters 1–12
3. Mick Cope, "Leading the Organisation to Learn", FT/Prentice Hall, 1998

Chapter 2. Corruption and Closed Minds.

1. Kiell Nordstrom, Jonas Ridderstrale, "Funky Business", FT Paperback, London 2000, pps, 32, 39, 49, 55, 56, 113, 273
2. Satyajit Das, "Traders, Guns and Money", FT Prentice Hall 2006
3. *Financial Times*, 06/06/06
4. BrandChannel US Readers' Choice Award
5. See Chapter 3, note 1.
6. Malcolm Gladwell, "The Tipping Point: How Little Things Can Make A Difference", Abacus, 2006
7. Stories sourced from *The Times* and *MediaPlanet* Feb. 21ᵗ 2007

8. Third Global Congress on Counterfeiting and Piracy, January 2007
9. Operation Jupiter
10. Moses Naim, "Illicit", Heinemann, 2005
11. *The Sunday Times*, 11/13/06
12. Robert Baer, "See No Evil", Arrow Books, 2002, pps127, 350, 399
13. Graucho Marx
14. The Roper Centre for Public Opinion Research, August 2005
15. HDS Greenawat, *International Herald Tribune*, April 18, 2007
16. John Perkins, "Confessions of an Economic Hit Man", p179, Ebury Press, 2006
17. Aydinli and Rosenau, "Globalisation, Security and the Nation State".p 17, Profile Books, 2005
18. Louis de Thomas and Neal St Anthony , "Doing Right in a Shrinking World", Greenleaf , 2006, p33
19. Mr Ben Heineman, at the time of writing
20. Rachel Briggs and Charlie Edwards, "Risk Management Study 2006", Demos
21. Harvard Business Review, p 106, April 2007
22. Robert Baer, "See No Evil", Arrow Books, 2002, pps127, 350, 399
23. ibid.
24. ibid
25. Nassim Taleb, "The Black Swan", p192, Random House, 2007
26. Ibid
27. Karl Popper, Google Quotes Sources—
28. John Darwin, "After Tamerlane: The Global History of Empire", Allen Lane, Penguin Books, 2007

Chapter 3. A Fresh Start - Outset Security

1. Thomas L Friedmann, "The World is Flat", Farrar, Strauss & Giroux, 2005
2. Garner, ibid, p 289

Chapter 4. Making Security a Competitive Asset

1. Kevin Green, Burrill Green
2. David Burrill, Burrill Green
3. Nassim Taleb , "The Black Swan", Allen Lane, 2007
4. Questions and Answers based on a presentation developed by Professor John Quelch, Harvard University and former Dean of London Business School
5. H McCrae, " The World in 2020", Harvard Business School Press, 1994
6. Charles Leadbetter, *The Times*, 13/10/06
7. Phillip Bobbitt, Terror and Consent, 2008-11-04, Penguin Books, 2009
8. Bruce Schneier, "Beyond Fear", p 90, Copernicus Books, 2003
9. Francis Fukuyama, *The Times*. October 14 2008-11-04
10. Young & Rubicam, "Brand Asset Valuator", 1989
11. H Sebag Montefiore, *The Sunday Times*, 04/06/06
12. 9/11 Commission Report, p 339
13. ibid. p 352
14. Thomas C Schelling, "Bush on War", p 23
15. Charles Dickens, "Hard Times "

16. Nassim Taleb, "The Black Swan", p144, Allen Lane, 2007
17. Admiral Bill Owens, "Lifting the Fog of War", Farrar, Strauss & giroux, 2000
18. PC David Copperfield, "Wasting Police Time",pps 23, 103, 104, 108, 163, Monday Books, 2006,
19. G Weimann, "Terror on the Internet", US IOP, 2006
20. Nassim Taleb, "The Black Swan", Allen Lane, 2007

Chapter 5. Security and Shareholder Value

1. H McCrae, "The World in 2020", Harvard Business School Press, 1994
2. Chris Anderson, "The Long Tail", 2006
3. A van Agtmael, "The Emerging Markets Century", see Chapter 1, note 2
4. Deutsche Bank/Booz Allen Hamilton, Proprietary Research
5. A Hilton, "The Evening Standard", City Comment, 2006
6. B Jopson, *Financial Times*, 08/06/06

Chapter 6. Getting Even More from Your Investment in Security

1. Bruce Schneier, "Beyond Fear", Springer, 2006
2. Steven D Levitt & Stephen J Dubner, "Freakonomics", Penguin Books, 2005
3. Kevin Mitnick, "The Art of Deception", Wiley 2002
4. Robert Cialdini, "Influence: The Psychology of Persuasion", 2007"
5. FBI Survey, April 2002
6. Niklaus Wirth, Wikipedia quotes 2007
7. Tim Koller, *Financial Times*, 10/06/06
8. Eccles/Lane/Wilson, *Harvard Business Review* 1999
9. John Roberts, "The Modern Firm", Oxford University Press, 2004
10. MarkL Sirower, "The Synergy Trap: How Companies Lose the Acquisition Game", 1997
11. John Cole, Partner, Ernst & Young, 21/01/07
12. *The Director* magazine, November 2006
13. Adrian Jones, commentator, Wiggin
14. *The Economist*, Feb 2 2007

Chapter 7. Achieving A Secure Advantage

1. Eric Hobsbawm, "The Short Twentieth Century", Abacus 1994
2. Thomas L Friedmann, "The World is Flat", p113, 215, Penguin 2005
3. Antoine van Agtmael, "The Emerging Markets Century", Simon & Schuster 2007
4. Niall Ferguson, "The Pity of War", Penguin Books

Chapter 8. Making Security Make Sense

1. Kiell Nordstrom, Jonas Ridderstrale, "Funky Business", FT Paperback, London 2000, (see Chapter 2, note 1)
2. John Cooper Clarke, "Don't", for "The Independent" Newspaper TV Commercial
3. M Cope (see above, Chapter 1, note 3)

Chapter 9. Security Leadership

1. Eric Hobsbawm (see above Chapter 7, note 1)
2. T S Eliot, " Burnt Norton", Four Quartets, Faber & Faber

3. Henry Mintzberg, "Developing Managers not MBA's", FT Prentice Hall, 2004
4. "Managing in an Unpredictable World", London Business School Course, Professor Donald Sull, LBS & Harvard University
5. ibid
6. *The Economist*, September 2003
7. Daniel H Pink, "A Whole New Mind: Moving from the Information Age to the Conceptual Age, Paperback, 2008
8. P Babiak, R D Hare, "Snakes in Suits" p 135, Harper Collins, 2006
9. *Sunday Times*, 08/10/06
10. Mark Gerzon, "Leading through Conflict", Harvard Business Scool Press, 2006

Chapter 10. Further Perspectives on the Changing Role of Corporate Security

1. *Financial Times*, April 18 2007
2. 2. Google quotes, "Einstein Principle"

Chapter 11. Standards in Security. Do You Measure Up?

1. Burrill Green is indebted to the Security Executive Council, Washington, USA, for its work in metrics and measurement. See www.securityexecutivecouncil.com for more on this key strategic resource. Title quote from George Campbell, "Measures and Metrics in Corporate Security"
2. "USA Today", May 19, 2006

Chapter 12. Designing a Profitable Multi-Function Security Organisation

1. John Roberts, "The Modern Firm", Oxford University Press, 2004
2. Thomas L Friedmann,"The World is Flat", p359, Farrar, Strauss & Giroux, 2005
3. *Financial Times*, 17/11/06
4. Cass R Sunstein, "Infotopia",.pps. 60, 65, 69, 85, 102, 198, Oxford University Press, 2006
5. J Sonnenfeld, "What makes great Boards", Harvard Business Review Sept 2002

Chapter 13. Security as a Brand

1. Francis Fukuyama, "Trust: The Social Virtues and the Creation of Prosperity", The Free Press, 1995"
2. Laermer & Simmons, "Punk Marketing", Collins 2007

Acknowledgements and Notes

This book captures the thinking and practice of the Burrill Green Limited management consulting company, and its specialised work in corporate security. Burrill Green practises what it espouses, and all Burrill Green Associates have long-term proven successes in their fields. We have theoreticians, but all are also practitioners. To those associates, first, we say thank you for their experience and significant contributions to this work.

To the many specialists and supporters in other fields who have given us insights and anecdotes, experience and counsel, enabling this book to become a reality, our thanks also extend deeply to them.

To our families and friends who enabled us to have these experiences, and who gave unconditional support and encouragement, we offer our thanks and love.

The work goes on.....

"Kevin Oschner of Columbia University has a scanner that renders meticulous maps of how the brain reacts to specific stimulus, be it a photo of someone in terror, or, via headphones, a baby's laugh. Imaging studies using these methods have allowed neuroscientists to chart with unprecedented precision the zones of the brain that intertwine in orchestrated action during the vast number of person-person encounters". Imagine the input of miniaturisation, and in thirty years there'll be a handheld device that lets you read how your colleague truly responds to stimuli. Privacy really is going to face some challenges then.

(Daniel Goleman, "Social Intelligence: The New Science of Social Relationships", p.75, 2007).

Of the 500 largest US companies in 1957, only 74 were still part of that select organisation, the Standard and Poor's 500, 40 years later. Only a few had disappeared in mergers – the rest either shrunk or went bust.

The person who was trained to regard the Cold War as the biggest threat to mankind was also trained to look at threats and risks in ways that would enable him to handle unpredictable developments in years to come. The nature of risk remains a fundamental aspect of the human condition. What changes are the names and places that constitute risk, while the underlying drivers have constants.

On this basis, it is worth thinking a little further about the next set of names and places that will constitute risk to someone, somewhere, and opportunity to someone and some where else. As usual, it all depends on where you stand, what you see, and what your perspective is.

Antoine van Agtmael was an interrogator in the Dutch Army. He regarded this as a good experience when attempting to sort the wheat from the chaff while deciphering and discounting 'often inscrutable management spin'. He became the investment manager pioneer who coined the term 'emerging markets', and has for years run the company Emerging Markets Management LLC. Here are some of his thoughts to stimulate the security value seeker of the near future: the idea that world-class global competitors might come from 'emerging markets' was widely dismissed by the Western Establishment as being an absurd notion. But in the words of George Soros, successful investing takes advantage of the "gap between perception and reality". Often that gap may simply go by the name *prejudice*. Emerging multinationals with currently #1 global market shares in their applications include Samsung Electronics, TSMC Taiwan, Hon Hai Taiwan, Asustek Taiwan, Quanta Taiwan, Embraer Brasil, Tenaris Argentina, Hyundai Heavy Korea, and Yue Yuen China. Other major players are growing daily, like Tata group out of India. New world-class security leaders are increasingly likely to be reading this book in English as their second or third language, but be just as acquainted with it in their own language versions. As we noted, Van Agtmael's empirical observations led him to conclude that the primary success drivers for these companies have also been different from general perception. 'Man-made' factors turn out to be more important than natural resources or the advantage of low-cost labour in determining whether a firm wins or loses over the long haul. It turns out that unconventional thinking, an ability to adapt to life-threatening crises, a global mind-set, and disciplined ambition are crucial ingredients for virtually all companies that succeed in attaining world-class status".

As Charles Darwin also noted, it is not the strongest of the species that survive, nor the most intelligent, but the ones most responsive to change.

Dig deeper, be curious, and keep an objective attitude.

Stay in touch...
www.burrillgreen.com and www.secureleadership.com